Terrific Tales to Tell

From the Storyknifing Tradition

By Valerie Marsh

Illustrated by Patrick K. Luzadder

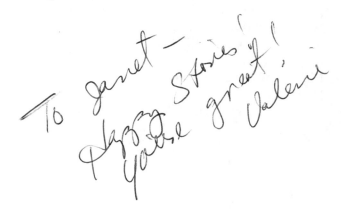

To Janet —
Happy Stories!
You're great!
Valerie

Alleyside Press®

Fort Atkinson, Wisconsin

Published by Alleyside Press,
an imprint of Highsmith Press LLC
Highsmith Press
W5527 Highway 106
P.O. Box 800
Fort Atkinson, Wisconsin 53538-0800
1-800-558-2110

© Valerie Marsh, 1997
Cover design: Frank Neu

The paper used in this publication meets the minimum requirements of American National Standard for Information Science — Permanence of Paper for Printed Library Material. ANSI/NISO Z39.48-1992.

Library of Congress Cataloging in Publication
Marsh, Valerie.
    Terrific tales to tell: from the storyknifing tradition / by Valerie Marsh ; illustrated by Patrick K. Luzadder.
    p. cm.
  ISBN 0-917846-60-5 (softcover)
  1. Storytelling. 2. Folklore–Study and teaching (Elementary). 3. Folklore and children. 4. Teaching–Aids and devices.
  I. Title.
GR72.3.M36 1997
372.64'2'044–dc20   96-43080
                                                        CIP

From life we each draw many distinctive and varied experiences. As we tell our daily adventures to friends and family, we make sense of them.

I dedicate this book to the most exciting draw and tell story of all —
LIFE.

Other books by Valerie Marsh

Beyond Words: Great Stories for Hand and Voice

Mystery-Fold: Stories to Tell, Draw and Fold

Paper-Cutting Stories from A to Z

Paper-Cutting Stories for Holidays and Special Events

Story Puzzles: Tales in the Tangram Tradition

Storyteller's Sampler

Contents

Introduction

Do you have a class full of doodlers? Kids are always drawing little pictures in the margins of their papers. You can help them turn their doodles and other drawings into stories with this technique called storyknifing.

There are many advantages to drawing while telling.

- It is an unusual way to tell a story—one that your listeners probably have not experienced before. Therefore it captures their immediate attention.

- It is a great focal point for you and your listeners.

- It is an easy technique for your listeners to learn and do themselves.

- It encourages creativity.

Sometimes the object that you are drawing is obvious. With other stories, however, the listeners may become so involved in the story that they're not aware of what the drawing is turning out to be until the end of the story. When this happens, storyknifing is even more fun because the listeners are surprised by the picture.

Why storytelling?

Storytelling is fun! Fun for the listeners and the teller! And one of the best ways to tell a great story is to be a storyteacher! As a storyteacher you are telling stories for many reasons—enjoyment, appreciation of good literature and development of listening skills, to name just a few. But most importantly, you are demonstrating to children how they themselves can tell stories. This takes the pressure off you to be a great performer. Instead, you are just doing what you probably do everyday, and that is work with children. When you think of it in this context, storytelling becomes easy. You are a storyteacher. Storyteaching has one main goal—to empower children to enjoy stories and to tell stories themselves.

Just by listening to your story, children develop higher level thinking skills, including critical thinking, short- and long-term memory, analysis, synthesis, and sequencing. Children also learn to distinguish between reality and fantasy. They gain general knowledge, a better understanding of other cultures, compassion, and self-confidence. Storylistening gives children a chance to develop their creative imagination! Finally, while listening to a story, the listeners and the teller can escape from the real world for a few moments, coming back to it with renewed vigor and increased confidence.

Always be sure to repeat favorite stories. Sometimes when a story is repeated, it will become a favorite, and each story deserves to be told at least twice. Of course, the best indicator of which stories to tell come from your audience, and a child's requests for a particular story should be honored whenever possible.

The stories here can be used with children of all ages. Some are very simple and familiar. After hearing the story once or twice, students can tell it all by themselves. Other stories have a much higher degree of sophistication and can be used to introduce discussions of more complex issues. Obviously, a twelve-year-old listener brings different experiences and expectations to the story than does a six-year-old. Each listener and teller gains what he needs from the story at a particular moment in his life.

When should you tell these stories?

- Rewards: Children need to learn that rewards can take forms other than materials things such as food, stickers, etc. Rewards can also be active entertainment rather that passive (such as a movie).

- Quiet times after recess or lunch.

- Waiting times between classes or during lunch periods.

- Holiday parties: Choose a story to entertain children at the party.

- Unexpected delays such as waiting for a late speaker during a school convocation.

- Entertainment at a school fair or carnival.

- After-school art and crafts programs.

- After-school child care programs.

- Curriculum integration of art, listening skills, sequencing skills, writing skills, history.

To guarantee your success

Using your imagination, you can come up with all kinds of ways to integrate wonderful stories into your work with children. A few simple tips guarantee a pleasurable, successful story session every time.

- Select an appropriate story for your listeners.

- Be familiar with the story and the drawing that goes with it.

- Have in mind some ideas for discussion after the story.

- Be ready to hear "Tell it again!"

- Enjoy yourself!

Celebrate life with a story!

What is storyknifing?

Storyknifing is an intriguing name and based in history. In the late nineteenth century, anthropologists and ethnologists discovered that the Inuit people told stories to each other while drawing pictures in the winter snow and summer mud. To draw their pictures they used a rounded knife made of whalebone. Their method of storytelling became known as storyknifing.

As you tell these stories you will be drawing a picture. Today you can use markers, chalk, or crayons! At the end of your story, you will also have completed your drawing. Your listeners will be surprised by your picture!

Why combine storytelling and storyknifing?

Telling a story while drawing a picture is a great way to completely capture your listeners' interest. This is an unusual approach to storytelling and a memorable one based in centuries of tradition.

Most children love to draw and spend lots of time at it. After listening to a storyknifing story, children will often take their own drawings and turn them into a story.

Do you need to be an artist or seasoned storyteller?

No! All you need to do is trace! The pictures are designed to be used with any size paper.

How to tell storyknifing stories:

1. First place a piece of paper over the picture in this book. Trace all lines lightly with a pencil. (Later on, you might want to let your listeners in on this secret.) Note where you will place the tape.

2. Drawing steps are loosely related to the story. As the character goes places or does something, you add a new line to your picture.

3. Practice telling your story while drawing so that it becomes natural to talk and draw at the same time. Becoming familiar with the story and the drawing allows you to present the story easily and develop a natural rapport with your listeners.

If you forget what comes next or get stuck in a story, ask the listeners to repeat what's happened thus far (giving you time to think) or suggest what could come next.

Do not tell the class what object you are drawing. After hearing a few stories, children will begin to try to figure out the object you are drawing before you are finished. You will be able to tell by a child's facial expression when he or she knows what it is that you are drawing. If you notice a listener just bursting to "spill" the answer, recognize him or her quietly with an aside such as "Shhh...it's a secret."

4. When you are storytelling to a large group, you'll want to tape the drawing paper to a wall. You can also use a chalkboard, overhead projector or dry erase board. You can enlarge the picture (use an opaque projector if you wish) to make it more easily seen. If you have just a few listeners, everyone could sit around a table.

5. Retell the story at least once. Retelling the story gives the listener a second chance to enjoy it as well as to learn the story and the drawing steps. Stories can and should be changed by each storyteller, and a story will be a little different each time it is told.

How you and your listeners can create your own storyknifing stories:

1. Decide on a story to tell. Then choose something to draw that is an integral part of the story. Or, choose an object to draw, then find or write a story involving that object. "How to Draw" books are available in most libraries and are great resource for ideas.

2. During the telling of your story, relate the drawing steps to the storyline. For example, as a character goes places or does things, add new lines to your picture.

3. This is a great time to teach the story elements. Every story needs the following:

   a. an introduction

   b. characters

   c. location or setting

   d. action or plot

   e. resolution of plot

4. If you feel the picture will be easily guessed while you are telling the story, draw your picture upside down or sideways.

5. Expect simple, imperfect drawings and stories from your students. Their stories might even be remarkably similar to one you have told. This is fine, and quite a compliment to you.

6. Plan to have several sheets of paper for each student. Encourage them to tell their story to themselves first and then to a friend. Students may prefer to work together in writing and telling their story. When they tell their story to you, you can help them "work the bugs out."

7. After several practices with small groups of friends, your storytellers will be ready to present to the rest of the class. After their presentation, you might want to present each child with a "Storyteller's Certificate" or another story told by you.

All Kisses, All Hugs, All Hugs

Has your mom ever dropped you off at a babysitter's house and then gone to work or to run some errands? I bet that has happened to all of us at one time or another.

I once knew a cute little boy named Jake. His mom always dropped him off at his babysitter's on her way to work. Every morning she drove Jake over the hill **(Draw 1, one eye.)** and around the curved street to the sitter's house **(Draw 2, ear.)**

Jake's mother loved to make up silly rhymes, and when they arrived at the sitter's house she would always swing the car door open **(Draw 3, mouth curve.)** and say, "Jake, this is what I always say, I hope you have a really nice day!" Then she would walk him up to the door and say another silly rhyme. She always said, "Come here, you little doodlebug, and please give me a big snug hug. And so I will not miss you, please do let me kiss you."

One day Jake's mom was so busy thinking of her rhymes that she DID forget to hug him goodbye. That made Jake feel as cross as a bear. **(Draw 4, two X's, leaving space in between.)**

Then, the next day, she hugged him so hard that his eyes felt like they were going to pop right out of his head. **(Draw 5, two O's, with X in between.)**

Then, the day after that, when she drove over the hill **(Draw 6, other eye.)** and around the curved street to his babysitter's house **(Draw 7, other ear.)**, Jake's mom said, "Jake, this is what I always say, I hope you have a really nice day!"

She swung the car door open **(Draw 8, nose.)**, helped Jake out of the car, and walked him up to the door. Then she said, "Come here, you little doodlebug, and please give me a big snug hug. And so I will not miss you, please do let me kiss you."

Not that silly rhyme again! Jake felt crosser than a bear **(Draw 9, X.)** He was especially cross when she kissed him two times and left a circle of lipstick on each of his cheeks. **(Draw 10, two circles.)**

"Jake, honey, doodlebug, sweetie pie! Why do you look so cross?" his mom asked him.

"I am cross because I am tired of that silly RHYME you say all the TIME," answered Jake.

"Jake, you just did it yourself. You made a rhyme. You made a rhyme with TIME. RHYME--TIME, get it? Now, I've got to go so I can get to work on time. Give me a kiss and a hug goodbye."

"Mom, I just did. Did you forget?" asked Jake.

"Oh, that's right. I even got lipstick on you. Here, let me rub it off," said his mom.

"Mom, I have a rhyme. When I say my rhyme, then you'll know to give me a kiss and a hug goodbye. Then you don't have to say your silly rhyme anymore, okay?" asked Jake.

"Great idea," said his mom. "What's the rhyme?"

Jake answered, "All kisses, all hugs, all hugs. All kisses, all hugs, all hugs." And he gave his mom a big smile. **(Draw 11, complete circle around face. Turn paper upside down to show smiling face.)**

Jake's mother started to tell him that his poem didn't really rhyme. But Jake was smiling so big that she just smiled back and went off to work.

Every day after that, when Jake kissed his mother goodbye, he said his rhyme to her.

O X O X O X O

☼ Discussion Starters

Look at this row of X's and O's. Has anyone ever written this to you on the bottom of a birthday card? Did you know that all these X's and O's mean "kisses and hugs"?

Tell about a time that you made up a silly rhyme. Can you make one up now?

All Kisses, All Hugs, All Hugs

10   4   5   4   5   9   10

O X O X O X O

Anansi the Spider Gets Into Trouble

A Retelling of a West African Folktale

(Cut paper into circle before telling story.)

To the Ashanti people of West Africa, Kwaku-Anansi is a spider who is a lovable trickster. He is shrewd and cunning and always making mischief. In this traditional tale, it is Anansi himself who tumbles into trouble.

Far ago, Anansi had six sons. Each had a very special skill and was named according to his skill. The first son was called See Trouble. He knew when there was trouble, even if it was a long way off. The next son was Road Builder. Do you know what he could he do?

The third son was River Drinker, the fourth was Animal Skinner, and the fifth was Stone Thrower. The last son was very soft, and so he was called Cushion.

One day Anansi had traveled far from home and was lost. He was searching for his way home, but he wasn't looking where he was going. He fell into the river and landed in the mouth of a fish.

At that exact moment, See Trouble called out, "Father Anansi is in trouble. I can see him." **(Draw 1, line inside paper's edge.)**

Immediately, Road Builder called out, "Follow me brothers! I will build a short road to father." **(Draw 2, second line around circle.)**

Soon See Trouble called out again, "There he is! Father Anansi is inside that fish."

River Drinker took a big drink, and then everyone saw the fish lying on the river bottom. **(Draw 3, fish.)** Animal Skinner opened the fish **(Draw 4, lines inside fish.)**, and Anansi climbed out. But just then, more trouble came. A big bird swooped down from the sky and snatched up Anansi with her beak. **(Draw 5, changing fish into a bird by drawing beak, wings and tail.)**

Stone Thrower picked up a rock and threw it at the bird. **(Color in 6, bird's eye.)**

Then Anansi was falling, falling through the sky. What would happen to him now? Cushion ran to help his father. He yelled, "Father, I am here. Fall on me. I am soft." **(Untape picture and wad up into a ball. Bounce lightly from hand to hand.)**

Anansi was safe at last. As they traveled home together, Anansi's six sons talked about how they had each played such an important role in rescuing their father. Then they began to argue about who was the bravest and most important son.

Anansi said to his sons, "When you all decide which of you is the bravest, please let me know. I would like to give him a present. I would like to give him my globe of white light, the one I found in the forest."

Anansi's sons argued so furiously that Anansi was afraid something would happen to the globe of white light. So he asked the god Nyame to help him. Anansi said, "Nyame, god of all things, please hold my globe of white light until this argument is over."

Nyame took the beautiful white light up into the sky with him for safekeeping. **(Smooth out the wad of paper and hold it over your head, plain side toward listeners.)**

Now, you know, to this very day Anansi's six sons are still arguing over who was the bravest in rescuing their father. And to this very day, Nyame is still holding the white light up in the sky. Everyone can see it. We call it the moon.

☼ **Discussion Starters**

There are many stories of how the moon got in the sky. Can you find one at the library? Perhaps you could write one of your own.

Anansi the Spider Gets Into Trouble

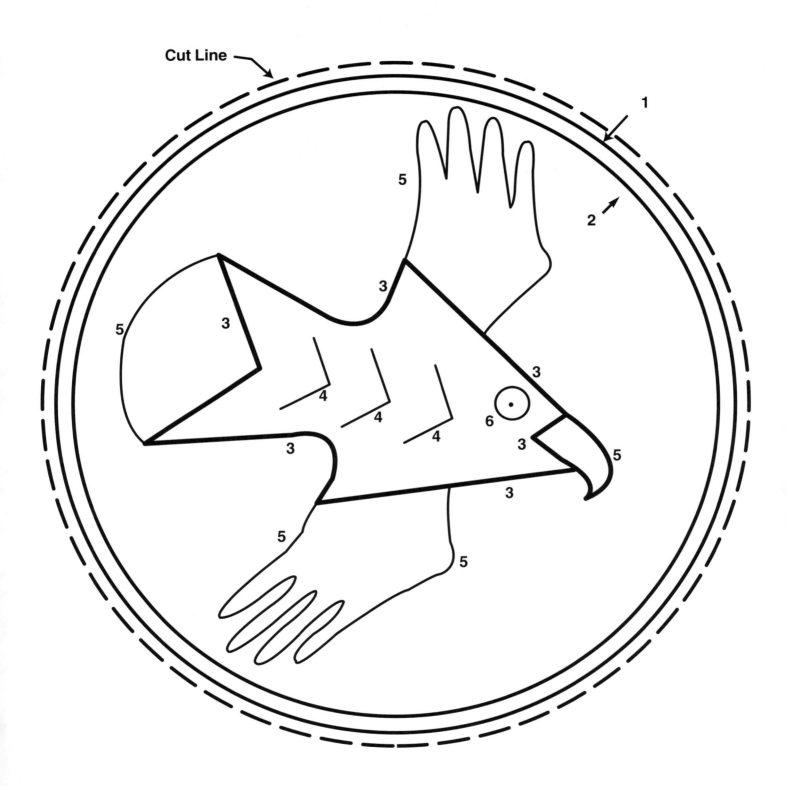

Cut Line

Cinderella

Far ago, there lived a rich man whose wife died suddenly. He was left alone to raise their only child, a beautiful daughter named Ella. One evening, Ella's father found her standing out in the cool night air, staring up at the half moon. **(Draw 1, half moon.)** She was crying.

Her father said, "Ella, before the next half moon, I will find you a new mother." **(Draw 2, half moon.)** He had heard of a widow in a distant land who had two daughters about Ella's age. The widow lived too far away for them to visit, so they exchanged friendly letters. **(Draw 3 and 4, rectangles.)**

Ella's father decided to marry the widow. She and her daughters traveled the great distance and arrived frowning and in a very bad mood. **(Draw 5, frowning eyebrows.)** Hoping for the best, he married her anyway.

It was a bad decision, and Ella's father was very unhappy. Soon after the wedding he died, leaving Ella alone with a mean stepmother and two very nasty stepsisters. **(Draw 6, faces of frowning stepsisters.)**

Immediately they turned Ella into a servant. She was forced to do all the cooking. **(Draw 7, bowl of food.)** Even though her hot food smelled and tasted delicious, the mean stepsisters constantly complained. **(Draw 8, steam from bowl.)**

They forced her to keep the fires burning, even in the summer. **(Draw 9, pole and fire.)** Ella was kept so busy that she hardly ever had time to take a bath and usually had dust and cinders in her hair. In fact, her stepsisters made fun of her sooty hair. They said, "Look at Ella. She is covered with cinders. Let's call her Cinderella." They called her Cinderella so often that the name stuck, and soon everyone was calling her Cinderella.

One day a royal invitation to the Prince's ball was issued to all the maidens in the land. Cinderella wanted to go to the ball along with her stepsisters. But she had to spend so much time helping them get ready for the ball that she had no time to even think about a dress for herself.

That night as she sat sobbing to herself, her fairy godmother appeared. She immediately started helping Cinderella get ready for the ball. The fairy godmother had Cinderella running around getting all kinds of strange things, like mice, rats, and a large pumpkin.

Then the fairy godmother changed the pumpkin into a golden coach, the mice into horses, and the rat into a coachman. Last of all, she turned Cinderella's rags into a beautiful gown for the dance. She even gave Cinderella some beautiful glass slippers to fit her tiny feet. **(Draw 10, outline of slipper.)**

Before Cinderella left for the ball, her fairy godmother said, "Remember, child, leave the ball before midnight. For at midnight, the magic spell ends and everything changes back to the way it was before."

Cinderella had a wonderful time at the ball. She danced all evening with the Prince. Only when she heard the clock begin to strike midnight did Cinderella remember what her fairy godmother had said. She ran away from the Prince. In her haste to leave, one of her slippers fell off, but Cinderella could not take the time to pick it up.

The next day, the Prince proclaimed that he would marry the girl who could wear the tiny shoe. Every maiden in the land was to try it on.

When the Prince arrived at Cinderella's house, each of the stepsisters tried in vain to fit her foot into the shoe. Neither one could wear it. Finally, Cinderella asked, "May I please try on the shoe?"

Her stepsisters laughed at her and said, "You, a servant girl with cinders in your hair, want to try on the shoe!"

Nonetheless, Cinderella tried on the glass slipper, and it fit. Then she pulled the other slipper out of her apron pocket and slipped it on as well.

After taking some time to get to know each other, Cinderella and the Prince decided to get married. They returned to the Prince's castle and lived happily ever after. **(Turn drawing upside down and show castle.)**

☼ Discussion Starters

The story of Cinderella appears in many cultures. Each has its own unique variations. Compare and contrast some of these stories.

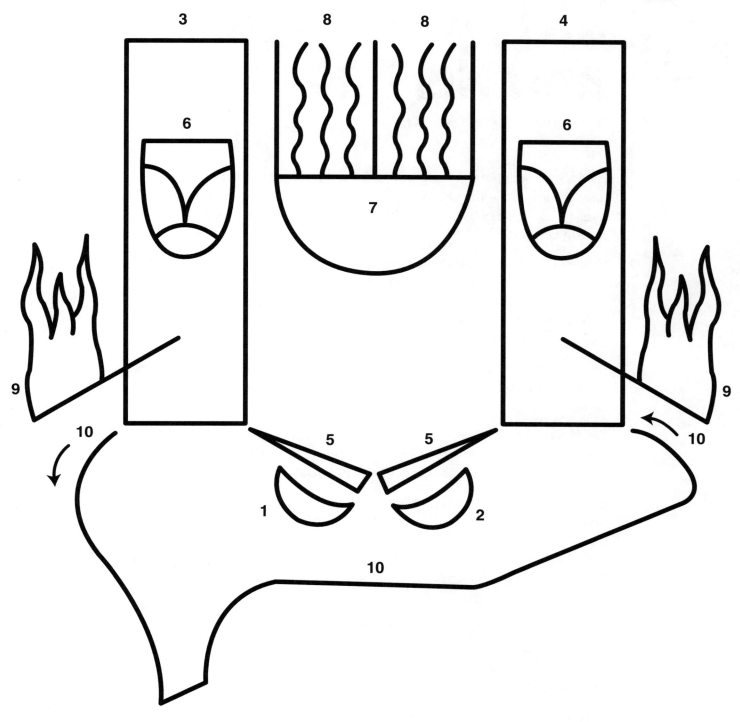

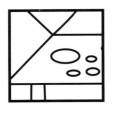

Dick Whittington and His Cat

A Traditional English Folktale

Far ago, a young English boy named Dick Whittington suddenly found himself all alone in the world. Dick's parents had died, and he had no relatives to take care of him. He decided to leave his village and seek his fortune in London.

When Dick got to London, he had no place to go and nothing to eat. He asked people walking by for spare coins so that he could buy food, but only a few people gave him coins. **(Draw 1, three large coins.)** Finally, he sat down in a doorway of a beautiful big house. The cook came out and yelled, "Be off with you! Now!"

Just then the owner of the house, Mr. Fitzwarren, came home and told the cook to feed Dick and give him some work to do around the kitchen. The unkind cook gave Dick all the worst jobs.

Dick's life was miserable because he had to work very long hours in the kitchen and sleep in an attic filled with rats. He could hear the rats scurrying back and forth all night long. **(Draw 2, two lines.)**

One day the master gave Dick a penny for shining his shoes. **(Add 3, another coin.)** Dick bought a cat with his penny. He took the cat home and hid her in his attic room. Every night, Dick would save part of his meager supper for his cat. But she didn't need much food because she was so good at hunting the rats in Dick's attic.

Not long after Dick had settled down in his new life, Mr. Fitzwarren called all of the servants to his parlor. He told them he was sending a ship out to trade with other countries and asked everyone what they wanted to invest in this voyage. It was the custom back then for everyone to put something of their own into a voyage.

When the master's daughter, Alice, saw that Dick did not have anything to invest in the voyage, she offered to give him some of her own money in his name. **(Draw 4, smaller coins.)**

But her father said that it had to be something of Dick's very own. So Dick went upstairs to get the only thing of value he had—his cat. **(Draw 5, trunk strap.)** Here is her tail.

When the cook saw how kind Alice was to Dick, she was meaner than ever to him, and he decided to run away. He set off very early in the morning and walked and walked. Just at daybreak he sat down to rest.

While he was resting, the bells of Bow Church started ringing. **(Draw 6, two bells.)** The bells seemed to say to him: "Turn again, Whittington, Thrice Lord Mayor of London."

Dick said to himself, "I'll be the Lord Mayor of London? Is that what the bells are saying to me? Is that what I'll be? In that case, I think I'll turn around and go back to Mr. Fitzwarren's kitchen. I won't let Cook's meanness bother me." Dick ran back as fast as he could and was working in the kitchen before Cook came down to prepare breakfast.

While Dick was having trouble with Cook, the master's ship, with Dick's cat on board, landed on the coast of Barbary. The King of Barbary invited the ship's captain to dinner at the palace. As soon as the servants brought in the food, rats and mice rushed in and devoured half the dinner before they could be chased away.

The captain sent one of his sailors to the ship to get Dick's cat. **(Draw 7, trunk strap.)** As soon as the cat was brought into the dining hall, she went to work and caught most of the rats and mice. The rest ran away in fear.

The king was so impressed that he offered to buy Dick's cat for a treasure chest of gold coins. The captain quickly agreed and the deal was done.

The ship sailed safely back to England. **(Draw 8, line.)** As soon as they arrived home, the captain went directly to Mr. Fitzwarren's house with the treasure chest of gold for Dick. Everyone was amazed when the captain said, "I sold Dick's cat to the King of Barbary. Here is his payment—a chest of gold coins." **(Draw 9, outline of treasure chest.)**

With his new fortune, Dick gave presents to everyone in the master's household, even Cook. Then he bought himself some new clothes and went to school. After a time, he married Alice, the master's daughter, and the bells at Bow Church rang again. Dick and Alice lived happily in London.

You know, Dick Whittington did become Lord Mayor of London three times. Each time he heard the bells ring, he remembered what they had said to him on the day that he had run away. His good fortune was all because of Dick's cat and the treasure chest of gold coins that she brought. **(Point again to the treasure chest.)**

☼ **Discussion Starters**

How do cats help us in today's world? Can you name some other animals that are very important to us? Has a pet or other animal ever brought you good luck?

21

Dick Whittington and His Cat

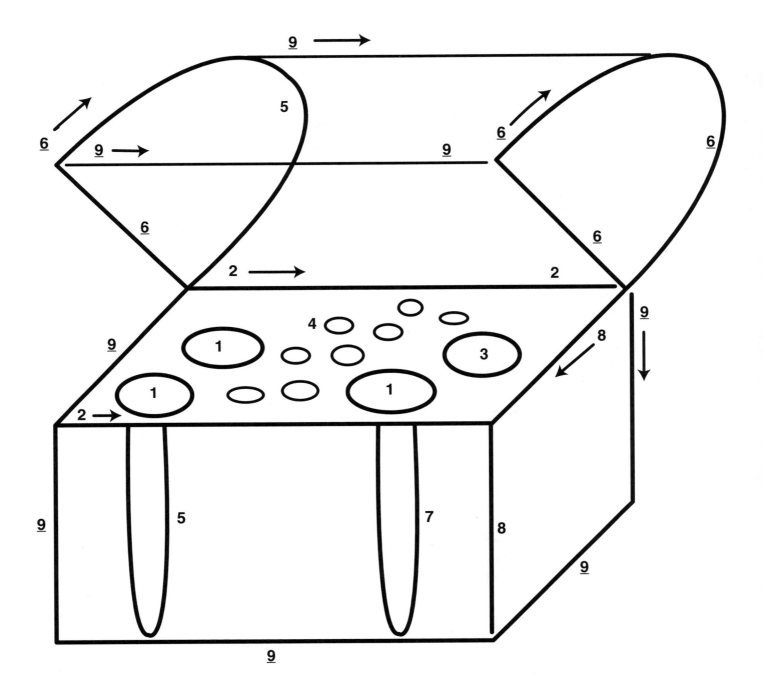

Dolphin Riddle

1. What waves all day but never says goodbye? The ocean
   (Draw 1, top back and tail fin.)

2. What is in the middle of a lake but never gets wet? An island
   (Draw 2, eye.)

3. What goes out into a lake but never comes back? A dock
   (Draw 3, bottom line of fish.)

4. What is used to steer in the water but never in the air? Fins
   (Draw 4, bottom and tail fins.)

5. What has scales but never weighs anything? Fish scales
   (Draw 5, scales on fish.)

6. What is a flower that you can write on? A lily pad
   (Draw 6, circle for head.)

Did you know that this **(point to drawing)** is a certain type of fish called
a dolphin fish? Why do you think it is called a dolphin fish? Does it
resemble the dolphins we see at the zoo?

Dolphins

D is for these delightful animals.

O is for the ocean where they live.

L is for the love they give to all.

P is for their peeps--they're talkative.

H is for their hands--just friendly fins.

I is for the interest they receive.

N is for their nose--it feels like pigskin.

S is for their smiles--they never leave.

Put them all together they spell DOLPHINS –
the mammals that mean the most to me.

☼ **Discussion Starters**

*Encourage your listeners to choose a favorite animal and make up a riddle
or poem about it. Try it using the letters as in the sample above.*

Dolphin Riddle

(Top of page when presenting)

Dolphin Fish

Goldilocks & the Three Bears' Lessons

How many of you have heard the famous story of "Goldilocks and the Three Bears?" You probably heard it when you were very young. Do you remember what happened first in this story?

Yes, the three bears went out for a walk while their porridge cooled. But they made a big mistake, and this mistake is key to their entire story. The bears did not lock their door—they didn't even shut it as they left.

We all know what happened next in the story. Goldilocks walked right into the bears' kitchen and tasted all three bowls of porridge. She tasted Papa Bear's big bowl of porridge and said **(Say it with me.)** "This is too hot." **(Draw 1, big bowl.)** Then she tasted Mama Bear's medium bowl of porridge and said, "This bowl is too cold." **(Draw 2, medium bowl.)** Then she tasted Baby Bear's small bowl of porridge and said, "This is just right!" … and she ate it all. **(Draw 3, smallest bowl.)**

In the next part of the story, you remember that Goldilocks went into the living room and sat down in the biggest chair. Do you remember whose chair that was? Yes, it was Papa Bear's chair. Goldilocks said, "This chair is too hard." **(Draw 4, largest chair.)** Then Goldilocks sat down in Mama Bear's chair **(Draw 5, medium chair.)** She said, "This chair is too soft." Then Goldilocks sat down in Baby Bear's chair and said, "This chair is just right." But do you remember what happened to the chair? Yes, it broke! **(Draw 6, smallest chair.)**

Finally, Goldilocks went into the bedroom. She lay down on the big bed, Papa Bear's bed, and said, "This bed is too hard." **(Draw 7, big bed.)** Then she lay down on the medium-size bed and said, "This bed is too soft." **(Draw 8, medium bed.)** Finally, she lay down on the smallest bed and said, "This bed is just right." She fell asleep. **(Draw 9, smallest bed.)**

The three bears came home and walked into their house. Papa Bear said, "Someone's been eating my porridge."

Mama Bear said, "Someone's been eating my porridge."

Baby Bear said, "Someone's been eating my porridge and they ate it all up."

The three bears went into the living room. Papa Bear said, "Someone's been sitting in my chair."

Mama Bear said, "Someone's been sitting in my chair."

Baby Bear said, "Someone's been sitting in my chair and it's broken all to pieces."

The three bears went into their bedroom. Papa Bear said, "Someone's been sleeping in my bed."

Mama Bear said, "Someone's been sleeping in my bed."

Baby Bear said, "Someone's been sleeping in my bed, and there she is." With that, Goldilocks woke up and ran out of the three bears' house.

But this particular story about the bowls and the chairs and the beds has been told backwards all these years. Goldilocks has been unfairly blamed for intruding into the house of strangers, eating their food without their permission, breaking their furniture, and making herself at home to the point of even sleeping in their beds! But here's what really happened.

The morning that the bears left their kitchen door open and decided to go for a walk is the same morning that Goldilocks decided to make her career dream come true. Do you know what Goldilocks had always wanted to do with her life? She had always wanted to clean houses. Since she was very young, she had helped her mom with the housecleaning and she was very good at it. Now that Goldilocks was older, she decided to take the advice that her mama had always given her—"Just go out and do it."

So Goldilocks set off through the woods looking for a house to clean. And the first house that she came to was…yes, it was the house of the three bears. She looked in through the open kitchen door and called, "Hello, My name is Goldilocks. I'm looking for a house to clean. I was wondering if you would be interested. Hello? Anyone home?"

Of course, no one answered Goldilocks, so she walked right in. She saw that the kitchen was a big mess. The breakfast dishes were still sitting on the table. There was a dirty pan on the stove. There was a lot to do in the kitchen!

Then Goldilocks walked into the living room. All the chairs were scattered around. Yes, this room definitely needed straightening up.

Finally, she checked out the bedroom. The beds were all unmade, blankets everywhere. Another mess! Goldilocks said to herself, "This family definitely needs a great housecleaner like me. I'll get started right now!"

So Goldilocks started with the bedroom. She made the big bed. **(Retrace 7, big bed. Use a second color if desired.)** She made the medium bed. **(Retrace 8, medium bed.)** But Goldilocks could not find any more clean sheets for the smallest bed. **(Retrace 9, smallest bed.)** So she threw all the sheets into the washer and started cleaning in the living room while the sheets were in the washing machine.

She vacuumed, dusted, and straightened the chairs. **(Retrace 4, and 5, large and medium chairs.)** But the smallest chair was so beat up that it completely fell apart when she picked it up to vacuum under it. **(Retrace 6, smallest chair.)**

Then Goldilocks walked back to the kitchen. **(Draw 10, double line.)** She wiped off the counters, put away the food, and washed the pan and the small bowl. **(Retrace 3, small bowl.)** She had just started to wash the other two bowls **(Retrace 1 and 2, large and medium bowls.)** when the three bears walked in.

Goldilocks was so surprised that it was a family of bears who lived in the house that she ran out of their house and never came back. **(Draw 11, back of key.)**

Both Goldilocks and the Bear family learned lessons that day. Do you know what Goldilocks learned? She learned that she should always meet her customers and get their permission before cleaning their houses.

And what did the three bears learn? They learned to always lock their door and take something with them. Do you know what it might be?…yes, their KEY! **(Draw 12, circle at end of key.)**

☼ Discussion Starters

This story presents us with a different view point. Let's think of another story that we can tell from a different angle. What about "The Three Billy Goats Gruff" or "Little Red Riding Hood"? What would these stories be like if the troll or the wolf told them?

Goldilocks and the Three Bears

(Top of page when telling)

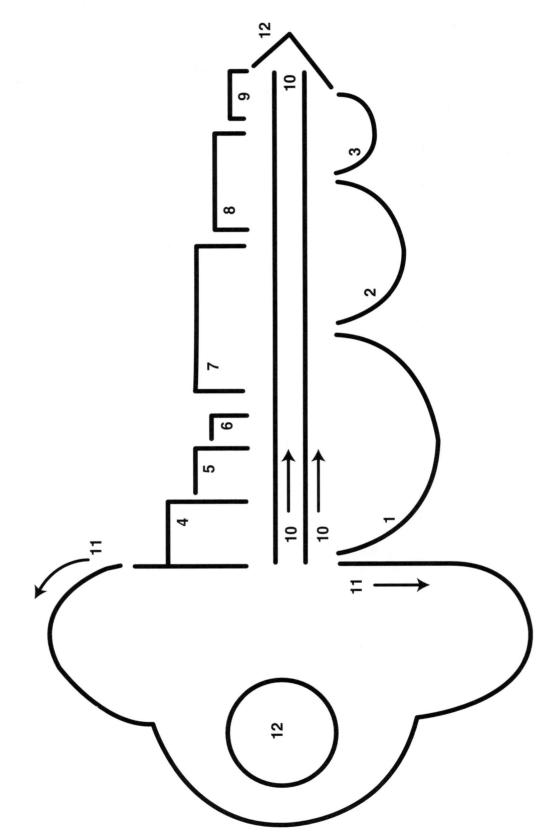

Grandma's Flower Garden

When I was a young girl, I lived very near my grandma and grandpa. I would walk or ride my bike to their house almost every day. I never knew what Grandma would be doing when I got to her house, but I knew she would be doing SOMETHING because she was always busy!

Of course, I always hoped that she would be taking my favorite chocolate chip cookies out of her oven. **(Draw 1, circles with dots.)** She always put them on the counter to cool. **(Draw 2, line.)**

My grandma was always doing things for her family. She knitted an afghan for each of her grandchildren and baby blankets for any relative who had a new baby. She would sit in her living room on hot summer evenings and knit while my grandpa watched the baseball games on TV. Her needles would click, click, and the rows and rows of knitting would come off her needles. **(Draw 3, lines down from line 2 and centered under cookies.)**

Every Sunday she would make a big dinner for us. She cooked all kinds of delicious dishes—homemade macaroni and cheese, fresh apple pie, and chocolate pudding. **(Draw 4, ovals.)**

She taught me how to sew when I was about eleven years old. My stitches were awkward and clumsy when I tried to sew two pieces of material together. **(Draw 5, two lines.)** I pushed my needle up and down through the material. **(Draw 6.)** But my stitches were so loose that the material would not even hold together. **(Draw 7.)** I was really frustrated with myself, but my grandma just smiled and said to keep practicing. She was good at smiling and at helping other people turn their frowns into smiles. **(Draw 8, frown, and 9, smiles.)**

But the main thing that my grandma was known for was her flower garden. **(Turn picture upside down to reveal garden.)** Every spring, she would plant all kinds of flower seeds, and the seeds would push their way through the warm brown earth. **(Draw 10, squiggly roots.)** Grandma would go out every day and water the seedlings and pull the weeds. Soon flowers would appear. **(Draw 11, extra petals.)** Leaves would grow. **(Draw 12, leaves.)** Her flower garden was on a very busy street corner, and everyone who passed by there just had to smile at its beauty.

Well, the years passed all too quickly, and my grandma finally became too old to plant her beautiful flower garden. Her house was sold to strangers. But, believe it or not, those strangers planted a flower garden on the exact same corner! Occasionally, I pass by that second flower garden. If I look very closely, I can still see a little old lady bending over and tending her flowers. **(Point to lady bent over.)**

☼ Discussion Starters

Do you have a special relative or friend who does nice things for you? Tell us about it. Can you create a picture about this?

(Top of page to start drawing)

Grandma's Flower Garden

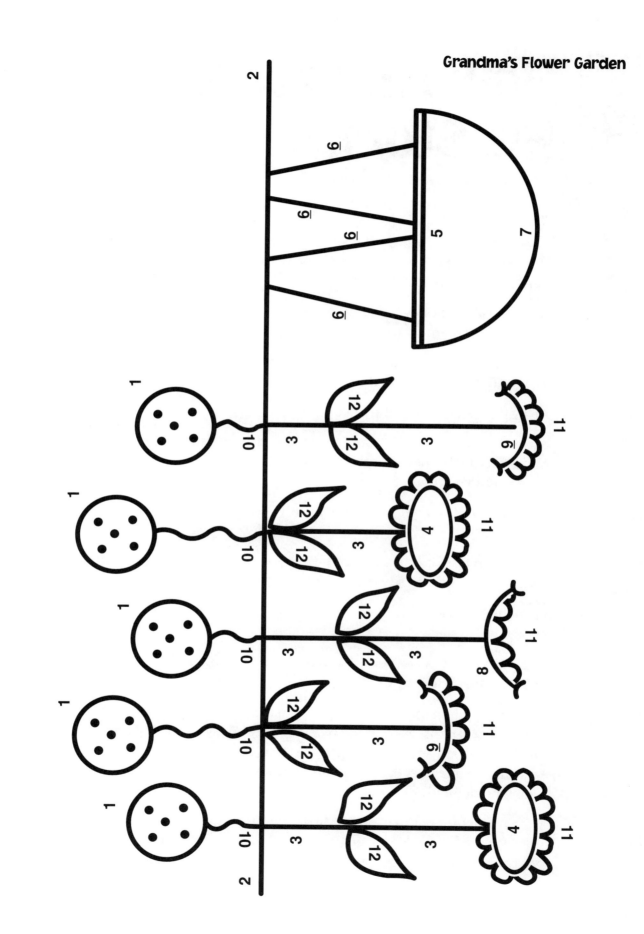

How Anansi Got His Stories

A Retelling of a West African Folktale

Kwaku-Anansi is a spider who keeps the stories for the Ashanti people of West Africa. He has the stories now, but he didn't always have them. Here's how Anansi got his stories.

Anansi wanted stories for his own, so he asked Sky God Nyamkonpon if he could buy them.

Nyamkonpon said, "I have not sold my stories to even the richest village. The price is too high."

Anansi asked, "What is the price?"

Nyamkonpon replied, "I want Onini the python, Osebo the leopard, Mmoboro the hornet swarm, and Mmoatia the spirit. But I don't think that you can get them for me."

Anansi said, "I will get them for you and I will give you my mother, Nsia, too."

Anansi and his wife cut a branch from a palm tree and a length of vine. **(Draw 1, line.)** Then they pretended to argue.

Onini the python came over and asked, "What are you two arguing about?"

Anansi said, "My wife, Aso, thinks that you are longer than this branch and I say that you are not."

Onini the python said, "I am longer than the palm branch. Watch this." He stretched himself along the branch. **(Draw 2, eye and body of snake.)** As soon as he did, Anansi and Aso quickly tied him to the branch with the vine. **(Draw 3, curved lines.)** Anansi had captured Onini the python!

Then Anansi set out to capture Mmoboro the hornet swarm. He cut a gourd and filled it with water. **(Draw 4, U-shape.)** Then he carried the gourd over to the hornets and poured half the water on them and half on himself. He yelled, "Hornets, don't you know it is raining? Come on into my gourd and keep dry." They all buzzed into the gourd. **(Draw 5, circles-including open circles for future eyes and mouth.)** As soon as they were all inside, Anansi slapped a plantain leaf over the gourd's opening and trapped the hornets. **(Draw 6, line over oval.)** Anansi had captured Mmoboro the hornet swarm!

Then Anansi dug a pit right in the middle of Osebo the leopard's path. In the morning, leopard was at the bottom of the pit, and he was angry! **(Draw 7, leopard's ears. Color in eyes, mouth.)** Anansi had captured Osebo the leopard!

Finally, Anansi set out to catch the spirit Mmoatia. He carved a wooden doll and covered it with sticky tree gum. Then he put a bowl of delicious yams in front of the carving. Soon Mmoatia came by and saw the yams. She asked, "Can I please have some yams?"

The carving did not reply, and so Mmoatia slapped the doll. When she did, her hand got stuck to the wood! **(Draw 8, leg.)** Then she hit it with her other hand, which also got stuck. **(Draw 9, leg.)** Then she kicked it. Her foot got stuck! **(Draw 10, leg.)** She kicked it again and her other foot got stuck! **(Draw 11, leg.)** Anansi had captured Mmoatia the spirit!

At last Anansi went to Nyamkonpon and said, "You wanted Onini the python, Osebo the leopard, Mmoboro the hornet swarm, and Mmoatia the spirit. Here they are. Here is my mother too."

Nyamkonpon said, "Anansi, you have paid the price. Now I give you the gift of my stories. They will now be called Spider Stories." **(Draw 12, 13, 14, 15 legs.)**

Anansi the Spider now owns the stories, and here is Anansi. **(Show Anansi the spider.)**

☼ **Discussion Starters**

Anansi figured out some very clever ways to catch animals bigger than him. Let's think of some other animals Anansi could catch. How could he catch them? We can create a new story with our ideas.

How Anansi Got His Stories

(Top of page when drawing)

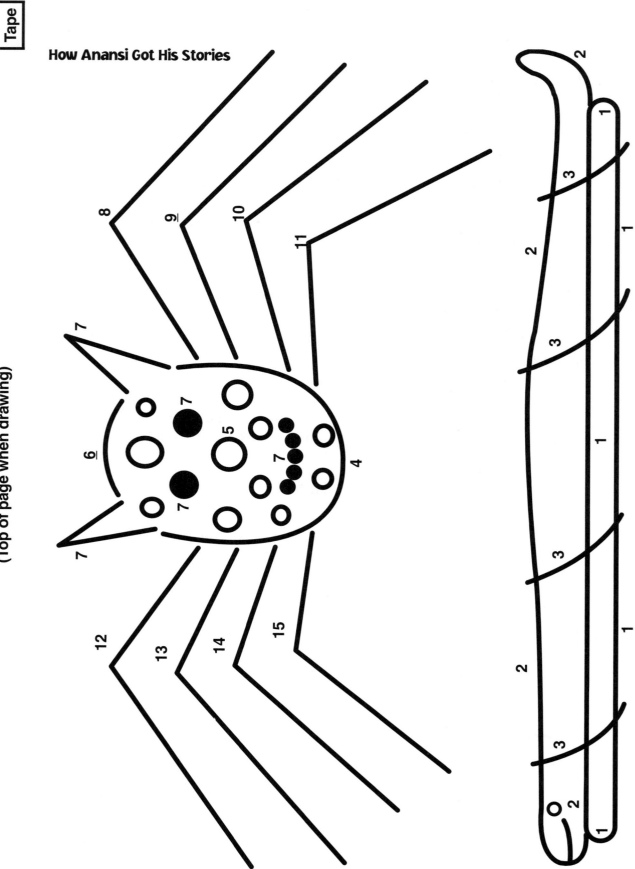

King Midas

A Greek Myth

Midas was a very rich king who loved gold. He spent all his time counting his gold coins and trying to figure out ways to get more. He stacked his coins higher and higher, into a bigger and bigger pile. The stack of coins was even taller than his daughter. **(Draw 1, coins.)**

One day, Bacchus, a Greek god, granted Midas one wish. Immediately, the king made his wish. He said, "I wish that everything I touch would turn to gold."

"Oh, do not wish for that. That wish will make you unhappy," said Bacchus.

"No, that is what I wish. I want to turn everything to gold just by my very touch," said Midas.

"Very well then, I will grant your wish," said Bacchus.

Midas was so happy. **(Draw 2, a smile.)** He decided to try out his wish. He touched two small trees at his feet and they turned to gold! **(Draw 3, sides of crown.)** He touched several stones on the ground and instantly they turned to gold! **(Draw 4, eyes and jewels in crown.)** He even touched a caterpillar crawling along the ground and—poof — gold! **(Draw 5, nose.)**

Then the king's daughter, whom he loved even more than gold, came running up to him. She kissed him and, as she did so, she too turned to gold! She was now the most beautiful golden statue in the land.

The king was very unhappy. **(Draw 6, sad mouth.)** He realized that his wish had been a very bad one. Now he would never be able to talk with his daughter again, to hug her, or to hear her sing.

He prayed to Bacchus. "Please, please, take back my wish. I do not want the golden touch anymore. I want my daughter back instead."

Bacchus said to Midas, "There is only one way to undo this wish. Follow this river all the way back to its beginnings. **(Draw 7, circle of face.)**

Jump into the water and wash away the golden magic. Then bring back a pitcher of water from the stream and pour it over your daughter."

King Midas traveled for days and days until he reached a pond at the river's source. He leapt into the pond, creating rings of waves. **(Point to 1, circles.)**

When he came out of the pond, the golden touch of King Midas had indeed been washed away. He returned home and poured a pitcher of the magical water on his daughter. **(Draw lines 8, top of crown. Turn drawing upside down to reveal king's face.)** The king was overjoyed as she sprang to life!

After that, whenever King Midas thought about gold, he told himself, "I will never again be greedy. I will always be satisfied with the gold and jewels in my crown." **(Draw 9, circles in eyes.)**

☼ **Discussion Starters**

King Midas did not choose a good wish. What would have been a better wish? If you could have one wish, what would it be?

The Miller and His Donkey

An Aesop's Fable

(Pre-cut, pre-fold, and lightly sketch figures before telling.)

Far ago, there lived a poor farmer and his son. **(Draw 1, boy and man.)** They were so poor, in fact, that they decided to sell their donkey in order to get money to buy food. He was a fine donkey, and they were sure he would bring a good price at the marketplace. **(Draw 2, donkey.)**

The miller, his son, and the donkey began the long walk to town very early the next morning. Very soon the sun rose high in the sky and it became very hot. As they stopped to drink from a small stream, some young girls playing in the stream began to laugh.

"What are you laughing at?" asked the miller's son.

"We are laughing because you and your father look so silly walking your donkey to town. You are silly to walk on such a hot day when you could ride your wonderful donkey instead," answered the girls.

The miller's son answered, "I think you are right. Very well then, I will ride on the donkey." And the miller's son got on the donkey. **(Fold 3, boy to center match line so he is on donkey.)**

A little farther down the road, they passed an old woman walking with a cane. As she passed them, she muttered something under her breath. But she said it just loud enough that they could hear her. She muttered, " What a terrible son he is to let his elderly father walk in this heat, while he rides in comfort upon the patient donkey."

Immediately the miller's son jumped off the donkey and said, "I think she is right. Here, father. You ride on the donkey awhile. You do look awfully hot." **(Unfold boy. Fold 4, father onto the donkey.)**

They continued on their way to town. The miller rode on the donkey, and his son walked beside him. Soon a traveler walking quickly to town overtook them. As he strode past them, he said, "Your donkey looks strong and sure-footed. You two would get to town faster if you both rode on the donkey."

"I think you are right," said the miller's son. And so he hopped back on the donkey. **(Fold 5, boy back onto the donkey.)**

Soon the three of them walked past a young woman carrying two baskets heavy with apples. She also had a baby in a baby carrier on her back. Her baby was fussing and trying to get out. As the miller and his son passed by, she said, "Shame on you both for making such a wonderful donkey carry such a heavy load on such a hot day! If anything, you two should be carrying it!"

"We think you are right," said the miller and his son. They felt so badly that they both immediately jumped down from the donkey. **(Unfold 6, both the father and boy.)** They tried to pick up the donkey to carry it to town. The miller picked up the donkey's front legs, and his son picked up the donkey's back legs. But the donkey kicked and brayed so much that it was impossible to carry the donkey anywhere at all.

A farmer working in his field nearby heard the loud commotion and walked over to offer his advice. He said, "If you are having trouble with your donkey, you should take a stick to it."

"We think you are right," replied the miller and his son. They looked around until they found a long, strong stick. After much struggling, they finally managed to tie the donkey to it. Now they could carry their donkey into town. **(Turn paper upside down and draw 7, stick through legs of donkey.)**

Finally, the miller and his son arrived in town, carrying their wonderful donkey upside down tied to a stick. They told everyone they met that their donkey was for sale. Many people had come to town that day in order to buy a donkey. But no one wanted to buy THIS donkey.

At the end of this long hot day, the hungry miller and his son finally turned around and began the long journey back to their home. They were still carrying their donkey upside down tied to the stick. And if they are not home yet, I guess they are still walking.

☼ Discussion Starters

Why do you think the miller and his son could not sell their donkey?

What do you think is the moral of this story? (You should base your decisions on common sense and your own preferences, instead of what other people think. If you try to please everyone, you may lose out in the end.)

The farmer said, "If you are having trouble with your donkey, you should take a stick to it." The miller interprets this statement literally. What do you think the farmer really meant by this? Are there other statements that we could take literally or figuratively? (Hit the nail on the head, slow as a turtle, etc.)

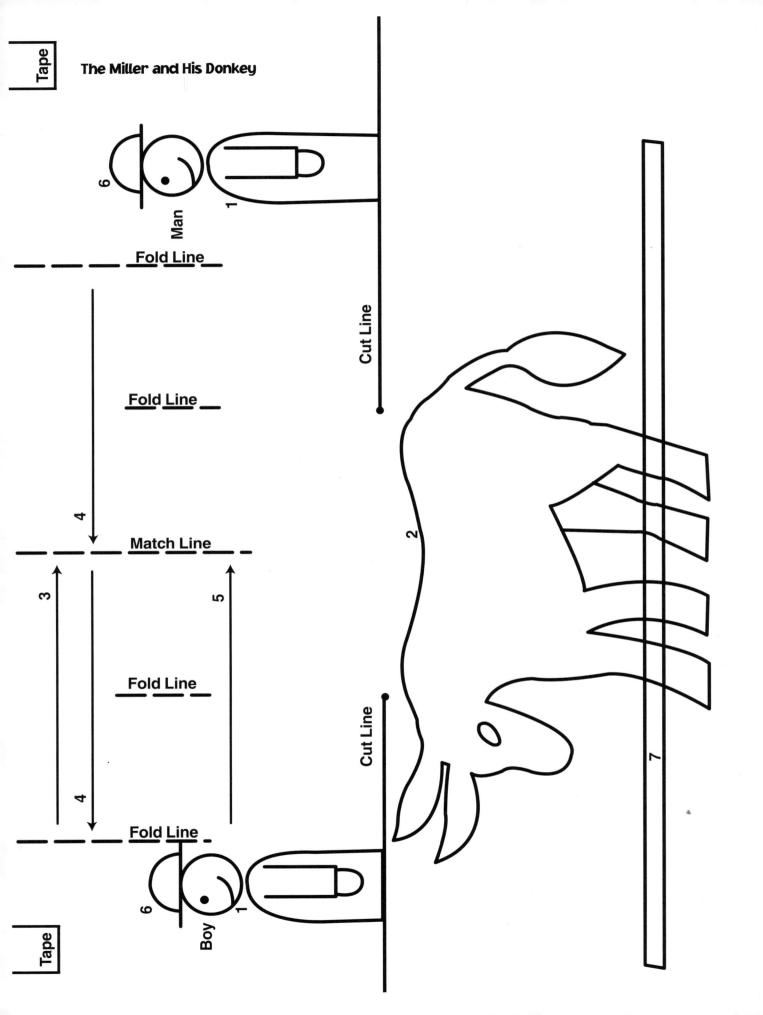

The Queen's Favorite Pet

An Asian Folktale

Once there was a queen who owned the most beautiful cat in the world. At least she thought it was the most beautiful cat in the world. The queen named her cat, Cat.

On Sunday, one of her servants said to the queen, "Your highness, your cat is as beautiful as the sun in the sky today."

The queen said, "My goodness, you are right. I shall name my cat, Sun. Cat is much too plain a name for such a beautiful animal. The sun floats above us and is always beautiful. From now on my cat shall be called Sun." **(Draw 1, eye.)**

On Monday, the queen ate her breakfast on the palace lawn. A different servant said to her, "Your highness, your cat, Sun, is more beautiful than the puffy white clouds floating above us. But your cat is not as powerful as the clouds, because right now the clouds are covering up the sun."

The queen said, "My goodness, you are right. The clouds cover up the sun. So I guess the clouds are more powerful than the sun. Therefore, I think I should change my cat's name from Sun to Cloud. From now on my beautiful cat shall be called Cloud." **(Draw 2, circle of head.)**

The Tuesday, third day, as the queen was eating lunch, a servant said, "Your highness, your cat, Cloud, is not as strong as the wind. Look how the wind blows the clouds about in the sky."

The queen said, "My goodness, you are right. I do not want the wind to be stronger than my cat, Cloud. The wind can blow the clouds about in the sky. So I think I should change my cat's name from Cloud to Wind. From now on my cat shall be called Wind." **(Draw 3, part of tail.)**

On Wednesday, as the queen ate dinner on the palace patio, another servant said to her, "Your highness, your cat, Wind, is stronger than the Clouds. But wind is not as sheltering as this wall. See how the wall stops the wind so that you may eat your dinner in peace. The wall shelters us from the strong wind."

The queen said, "My goodness, you are right. I do not think the wind is more sheltering than the wall. The wall shelters us from the strong wind. So I think I should change my cat's name from Wind to Wall. From now on my beautiful cat shall be called Wall." **(Draw 4, stripes.)**

On Thursday, as the queen sat on her patio quietly reading, a servant said to her, "Your highness, your cat, Wall, is more sheltering than the wind. But the wall is not as formidable as that mouse there. See how that little mouse is chewing holes all along the top of the wall. **(Draw 5, cat feet and base line.)** Why look there! I see a second mouse running all around and through the wall." **(Draw 6, other part of tail.)**

The queen said, "You are right. I do not think the wall is as formidable as a little mouse. So I think I should change my cat's name from Wall to Mouse. From now on my beautiful cat shall be called Mouse."

On Friday, as the queen strolled through her garden petting her cat, now named Mouse, a servant spoke to her. He said, "Your highness, your cat called Mouse is indeed more formidable than the wall."

Just then the cat, called Mouse, jumped off the queen's lap and chased the mouse who was running around the patio. **(Draw 7, body of cat.)** In no time at all, the cat had caught the mouse by his whiskers. **(Draw 8, nose and whiskers.)**

The queen exclaimed, "Look at that. My beautiful cat named Mouse has caught a mouse. That means that my cat is more extraordinary than the mouse. I think I should change my beautiful cat's name from Mouse to Cat. From now on, my cat shall be called Cat."

On Saturday, the seventh day, the queen announced a royal proclamation. It said, "From this day forward, all animals will be called by their rightful names. This includes my beautiful pet cat. He will be called Cat because that is the name he most deserves." **(Draw 9, second eye, and 10, ears. Turn drawing over with a flourish to reveal picture of cat.)**

>⋏< >⋏< >⋏<

☼ Discussion Starters

This story makes a circle, doesn't it? The cat starts out being called Cat and ends up being called Cat. In between, he gets called lots of other things. Can you think of some other names Cat could be called based on what he could do?

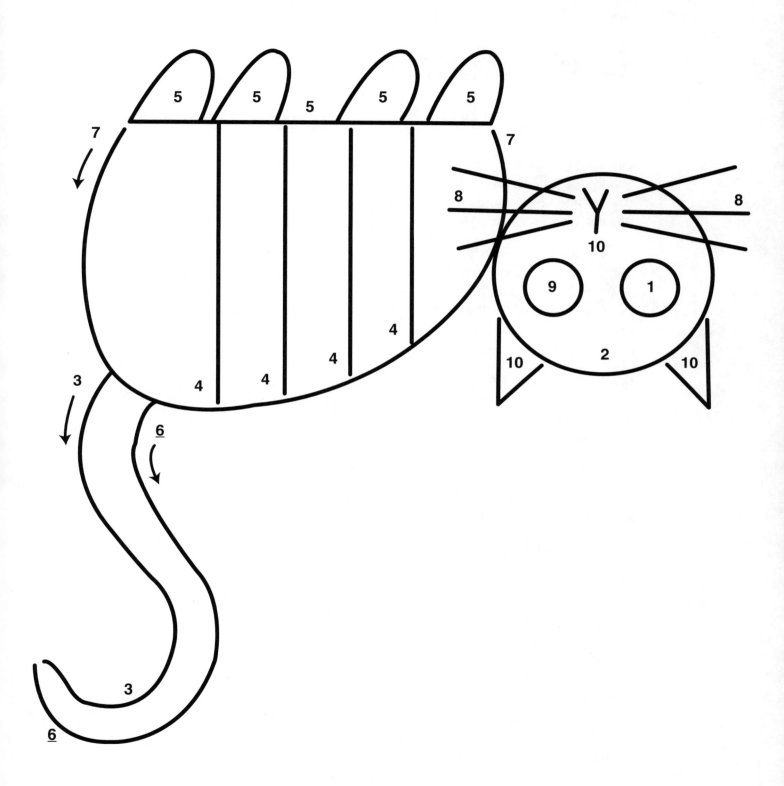

Shipwrecks, Rescues & Pirates

On Sunday, October 16, 1904, a terrible storm blew in near what is now Fort Pierce, Florida. The waters off the Atlantic coast of Florida were very dangerous during the gale. The waves got very high. **(Draw 1, double dip wave.)** They crashed in all directions. **(Draw 2, double dip waves.)**

A ship named the George Valentine was very near the coast. **(Draw 3, ship.)** This enormous 767-ton ship was from Italy and was carrying a heavy load of lumber. The strong winds ripped the Valentine's sails loose from the masts. **(Draw 4, mast poles.)** The ship was not able to sail. The billowing waves tossed the ship up and down and up and down. **(Draw 5, wave.)**

Finally, the ocean dashed the helpless ship against the rocks, and the ship exploded into thousands of pieces of lumber. **(Draw 6, pieces of wood.)** The sailors hung onto the pieces of wood for dear life. They yelled for someone to rescue them.

Were their voices heard above the roar of the storm?

Yes, a man named W.F. Rea heard the desperate cries for help. He set out to rescue the unfortunate sailors as they washed up to the beach.

This is what Mr. Rea wrote in his diary about the rescue:

> "The Valentine had a crew of 12. All were more or less injured—some severely. All totally exhausted and would have died before morning but for the timely assistance as none of the seven were able to stand when brought into the station—chilled through from exposure to the elements without clothing, and exhausted from hanging on to the riggings, battling with the waves that were one mass of floating lumber. Many were dashed against the rocks many times before I, the Keeper, could rescue them. I worked all night on the beach hunting through the lumber for disabled seamen. The air was full of flying lumber—the breaking of which sounding like the report of thousands of rifles."

Now, you are probably wondering who was W.F. Rea and what was he doing there in this terrible storm?

That's a good question. Here's the answer: W.F. Rea was the Keeper of the House of Refuge called Gilbert's Bar.

(Turn drawing over to reveal picture of house. Add 7, floor and roof lines.) This is Gilbert's Bar House of Refuge. Mr. Rea lived in this house. He was called the Keeper. The Keeper's job was to help shipwrecked sailors by giving them food, clothing and shelter until they could go back to their home.

That stormy night, Mr. Rea saved the lives of seven men, including the skipper of the Valentine, Captain Prospero. Keeper Rea rescued three Italians, two Swedes, one Scotsman, and one Russian.

Mr. Rea was very busy on the night of October 16, 1904. But he did not get to rest because the terrible storm that wrecked the Valentine continued on into the next day.

On Monday, October 17, 1904, a ship named the Cosme Colzadi ran ashore three miles north of Gilbert's Bar. One of the crewmen tied a rope to his body and swam ashore. Then the other fifteen sailors grabbed onto the rope and held onto it as they struggled through the pouring rain to shore.

A man named Harvey Baker, an African-American, helped all of the sailors into his house. Mr. Baker took care of them until the next morning when he brought them to Gilbert's Bar House of Refuge. Then there were twenty-two sailors that Keeper Rea was in charge of. He fixed them meals, gave them clothes and helped them if they were injured when their ship crashed. It was a very big job. The sailors stayed at his House of Refuge for thirteen days. Mr. Rea reported that he served the sailors a total of 159 meals!

Mr. Rea was one of twenty Keepers who were in charge of Gilbert's Bar House of Refuge over the course of seventy years. It was built in 1875, one of ten Houses of Refuge built along the Florida coast twenty to thirty miles apart.

Why was it called Gilbert's Bar House of Refuge? None of the Keepers were named Gilbert. Actually this house was named after Don Pedro Gilbert, a pirate who caused shipwrecks!

Don Pedro Gilbert was the son of a wealthy Spanish nobleman, but he did not want to earn his living honestly as a farmer or a merchant. Gilbert decided that being a pirate would be more fun, and he thought he could make lots of money—by stealing it. Pirate Gilbert bought a ship—low, sleek and fast—and painted it black. He put a narrow white stripe down the side and called his pirate ship the Panda.

Gilbert and his pirates made their headquarters on Hutchinson Island. This is where the House of Refuge was later built. **(Draw 8, door.)** The pirates hid their ship in the bay, where they cleaned it, repaired it and watched for passing ships.

When a ship sailed by that they thought they could capture, Gilbert and his pirates would light a small signal fire on the beach. **(Note burning wood in drawing.)** The captain of the ship would sail as close as possible to shore to see what the problem was. The unsuspecting captain didn't know that there was a reef just offshore, and his ship would crash into it. When the ship wrecked, Gilbert and his pirates would quickly jump in their boats, row out to the wreck and steal anything they could from the ship. This was a horrible crime, but the United States government did not have enough law enforcement officers to search out and capture the pirates.

Gilbert did this terrible trick so many times that the reef where the ships wrecked became known as Gilbert's Bar. When the lifesaving station was built on the island, people called it Gilbert's Bar House of Refuge. This is the only House of Refuge that still exists. It is listed on the National Register of Historic places and you can visit it today. It is a house built to do good things, but named after a ruthless pirate. **(Note house on drawing.)**

By the way, Gilbert and his fellow pirates were captured in 1833.

☼ **Discussion Starters**

The Keepers of the Bar risked their lives to help people. What other jobs can you think of that involve risk? You could write an exciting story about one of these jobs.

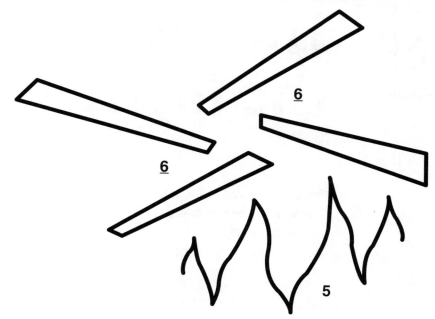

6

6

5

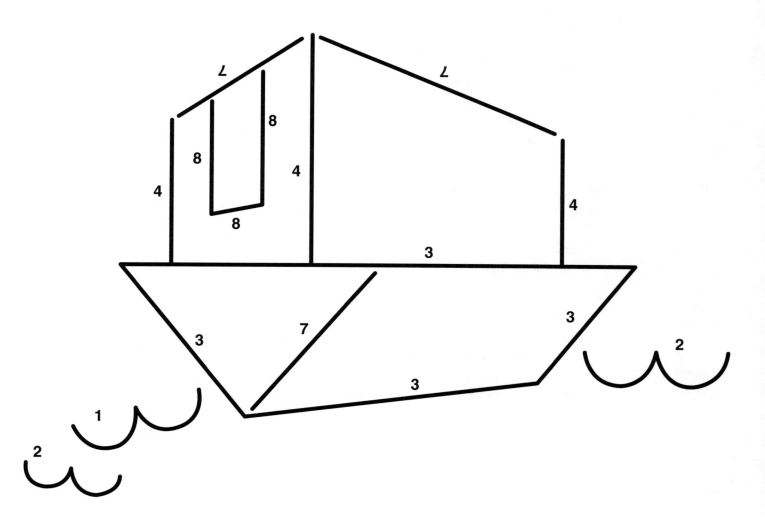

L

L

8

8

8

4

4

4

4

3

3

3

7

3

2

1

2

The Soldier and the Night

Once there was a gallant soldier who fought dragons and great beasts. **(Draw 1, armored helmet to represent soldier.)** He protected his people by drawing his strength from the sun. He loved the sun and stood tall, proud and strong in its light.

The soldier accomplished great things by the light of day, only to be overcome by the darkness of Night. When Night came upon the earth, the gallant soldier became sad. He was unable to do anything but sit in his house, alone and afraid. Night was his biggest enemy.

One day, he climbed a great mountain. As the sun set, the soldier reached the mountain's peak. **(Draw 2, mountain.)** He called out to his enemy, "Night, why do you cover the earth with darkness and gloom?"

Night answered by spitting great bolts of white lightning at him and roaring loudly. Then Night sent great torrents of rain down upon him. **(Draw 3, rain drops.)** This made the soldier very scared, very wet and very angry. Never had he had known an enemy who was so persistent. As he climbed down the mountain, the soldier decided that he would have to confront and defeat Night at all cost.

The next day, he and his horse rested and prepared for a long journey. **(Draw 4, horse.)** The following morning, he mounted his horse and rode along the ridge of the great mountain range, always climbing higher and higher. Soon he was high above the homes and fields. **(Draw 5, mountain ridge.)**

As he traveled, he thought about Night. He knew that at the end of every day Night would come and settle itself over the land like a great blanket. He could not get rid of Night. Since he could not get rid of it, he must overcome Night and his terrible fear of it. But how? Even now, Night was creeping in around him, sending its fingers of darkness around the trees and behind the bushes. Soon the world would be completely dark again.

The the soldier remembered how angry he had been when Night had sent its great bolts of white lightning down at him. **(Draw 6, lightning.)**

48

For a few seconds, the lightning had ripped Night apart. And the light had been so bright that it had hurt his eyes.

But wait, the lightning was bright, yet it came out of Night. Or did it? Maybe Night was hiding Daylight. Daylight could be trying to escape from behind Night. For a second, Daylight had come roaring out as lightning and thunder. But Night had immediately caught Daylight and covered it over again.

Then the soldier had a brilliant idea. Maybe Daylight needed rescuing. And rescuing was what this soldier did best. He should rescue Daylight from Night. But how?

By the time the soldier figured all this out, it was almost completely dark. He felt the old familiar stab of fear and turned his horse around to head back home. In the distance, he could hear the rumbling of Night. No wait, that wasn't Night—that was Daylight wanting to get out, calling him to come and rescue it. And here he was riding away like a coward.

He turned his horse around and yelled, "Never again! Never again will I be afraid of Night. Daylight, I am coming to rescue you!"

The soldier rode furiously along the mountain ridge, stabbing holes in Night with his long spear. **(Draw 7, spear.)** All night long he rode, stabbing the sky again and again until Night was filled with millions of tiny holes. He stabbed Night until he was so tired that he could no longer even lift his spear. Then, just before daybreak, the soldier collapsed in total exhaustion. He fell off his horse and rolled down the mountainside into the quiet valley below. **(Draw 8, armored helmet for soldier.)**

That sunny morning, a farmer discovered the soldier asleep in his field. He dragged the soldier over to the shade of a big tree. **(Draw 9, tree.)** All day long, the soldier slept in the shade.

Just as Night was creeping in and pushing out the daylight again, the soldier woke up. He moaned, "Here is black Night. I have lost the greatest battle of my life." He closed his eyes and tried to sleep again.

But the townspeople were not sleeping. They were all outside calling to each other and pointing to Night's sky. They were shouting, "Look! Look! Can you believe it! Oh, how beautiful! It is so beautiful!" **(Draw 10, stars halfway across sky.)**

They made so much noise that the soldier finally opened his eyes again to see what all the commotion was about. Instead of a completely dark night sky, he noticed a band of lights twinkling across it. The glistening lights stretched across the ridge where he had ridden the night before and stabbed so furiously at Night's sky. Now Night was absolutely beautiful, no longer depressing. It seemed to the soldier as if the lights were twinkling directly at him. "So I was right. Night was hiding Daylight behind it.

The soldier was no longer afraid of Night because he could see Daylight twinkling in the millions of tiny holes that he had jabbed in the sky. **(Draw 11, stars. Complete arc across sky.)** The townspeople were forever grateful. The gallant soldier had defeated the gloomy Night and created a beautiful band of white stars. Today, we know this wonder as the…Milky Way.

☼ Discussion Starters

Tell about a time that you were afraid of something and then conquered your fear.

The Soldier and the Night

Something from nothing

A Retelling of a Traditional Jewish Folktale

One day while they were sitting and waiting for supper to be ready, Matt asked a question to pass the time. He asked, "Uncle Loren, what is the best thing you own in the world?"

Uncle Loren thought for a moment and then answered, "It is nothing. Nothing at all."

"What do you mean, nothing?" asked Matt.

"The most precious thing I own is a memory. It is nothing now but a memory. Once, long ago, it was something, but now it is nothing. Let me tell you the story."

Uncle Loren settled back in his chair and began his story.

"When I was young, I spent my summers helping my mom and dad at their laundry. They had lots of laundry trucks that drove around town and picked up people's dirty laundry and delivered their clean clothes. When the trucks brought the dirty laundry in, it was my job to sort it out into piles of white and dark clothes. I also had to make sure that the clothes didn't get mixed up with anyone else's clothes. I'm fairly certain that it was in one of the laundry bins that I lost my most precious button." **(Draw 1, button.)**

"Your button?" asked Matt.

"Yes, I lost my button. But it didn't start out as a button. It started out as a blanket. It was my special blanket that my grandma made for me when I was a baby. It was a beautiful, soft, blue blanket." **(Draw 2, square outline.)**

"For my first three years, I carried that blanket around with me everywhere I went. I took it out with me to play, and of course I took it to bed with me every night. Finally, it got so worn around the edges that my mother asked me if she could sew something new for me from my old blanket."

52

"Something new from your old blanket?" asked Matt.

"Yes," answered Uncle Loren. "My mother was such a good seamstress. She sewed my old blanket into a comfortable new jacket for me. She told me that after she had snipped off the frayed edges of the blanket, there was just enough material left for a jacket." **(Draw 3, jacket.)**

"For the next three years, I wore that jacket everywhere I went. I even wore it in the summer when it was too hot to wear a jacket. Finally, it got so worn at the sleeves that my mother asked me if she could sew something new for me from my old jacket."

"Something new from your old jacket?" asked Matt.

"Yes," answered Uncle Loren. "My mother sewed my old jacket into a wonderful new vest for me. She told me that after she had snipped off the worn sleeves of the jacket, there was just enough material left for a vest." **(Draw 4, vest, double lines.)**

"For the next three years, and by then I was nine, I wore that vest everywhere I went. I wore it with my school clothes and even with my swim trunks. Finally, it got so worn at the sides that my mother asked me if she could sew something new for me from my old vest."

"Something new from your old vest?" asked Matt.

"Yes," answered Uncle Loren. "My mother sewed my old vest into a special new tie for me. She told me that after she had snipped off the worn sides of the vest, there was just enough material left for a tie." **(Draw 5, tie.)**

"For the next three years, I wore that tie everywhere I went. I wore my tie every day. Sometimes I would even tie it to a tree branch and swing on it. Finally, it got so worn at the bottom that my mother asked me if she could sew something new for me from my old tie."

"Something new from your old tie?" asked Matt.

"Yes," answered Uncle Loren. "My mother sewed my old tie into a handkerchief for me. She told me that after she had snipped off the worn part of the tie, there there was just enough left for a handkerchief." **(Draw 6, handkerchief–retrace rectangular top of tie.)**

"For the next three years, I carried that handkerchief in my pocket everywhere I went. I kept my cherished pocket watch wrapped up in it. Finally, it got so worn around the edges that my mother asked me if she could sew something new for me from my old handkerchief."

"Something new from your old handkerchief?" asked Matt.

"Yes," answered Uncle Loren. "My mother sewed my old handkerchief into a button for me. She told me that after she had snipped off the worn edges of the handkerchief, there was just enough left for a button." **(Color in 1, button.)**

"From then on, until the day I lost it, I wore that button everywhere I went. I wore it on my overalls and on my jeans. When I lost the button, I was very upset. But then I started thinking about all the things that button had been before it was a button. And as I was thinking, I remembered all of the things and people I had loved during the years I had my blanket, jacket, vest, tie, handkerchief, and button." **(Point to all the things as you name them.)**

"From my baby blanket, I had more than enough to make a memory. And even after my button was gone, I had just enough to make this story."

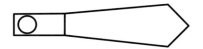

☼ Discussion Starters

Write a story about a good memory from your childhood. Can you draw a picture to go with your story?

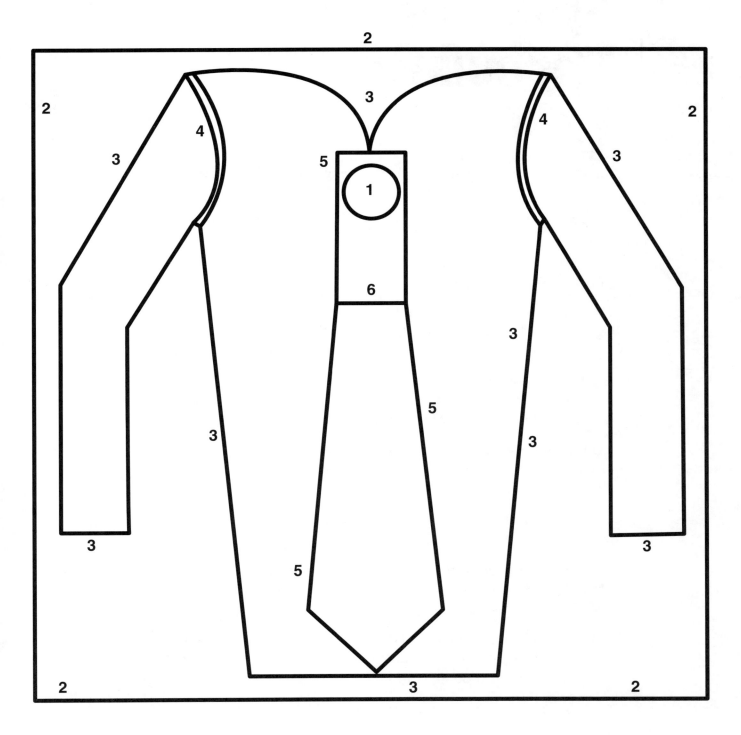

Sport of Spear Throwing

Far ago, children spent all their time playing games. They called their favorite game "spear throwing."

Here is how they played this game. Each child went down by the river and found a long stick. Then they sharpened their sticks to a point on one end. All the children gathered in a field, and one child drew a line in the dust. **(Draw 1, line.)**

Everyone stood behind the line. One child rolled a big, round rock across the field, and everyone threw their sticks at it. **(Draw 2, rock.)** The person who threw their spear closest to the rock was the winner.

The children played this spear throwing game so often that they became very good at it. They were happy when they were playing this game. But their mothers were not happy, not happy at all.

The mothers all said, "You children should spend your time at the river catching fish, instead of playing that silly game. At least if you catch fish, we will have something to eat."

"Oh, but we like this game. We really like throwing our spears in the open field," said the children.

"Tomorrow, you will all go down to the river and catch some fish for us. **(Draw 3, river.)** You will not play your spear throwing game tomorrow!" yelled all the mothers.

The very next day, when the children went outside, they headed directly to their field. They played spear throwing all day long. No one ever once thought about their mothers' request for them to go fishing.

That evening, the mothers were very angry. They all said, "We asked you to go down to the river to get some fish for supper. **(Draw 4, fish.)** We know that you think fishing is a hard job because it is so boring. But we need fish to eat. We did not want you to play spear throwing today. It is a waste of time. Not one of you obeyed our request. We are very unhappy about this."

56

The children all answered, "We are sorry. We will go fishing tomorrow. We will not play spear throwing tomorrow."

But the very next day, when the children went outside, they headed directly to their field. They played spear throwing all day long again. No one ever once thought about their mothers' request for them to go fishing.

That evening, the mothers were even more angry. They all said, "We asked you to go down to the river to get some fish for supper. **(Draw 5, fish.)** We did not want you to play spear throwing again today. It is a waste of time. But not one of you obeyed our request. We are very unhappy about this."

The mothers were so unhappy, in fact, that as soon as their children were asleep, the mothers threw all the sharpened sticks they could find into the river. **(Draw 6, sticks in water.)**

In the morning, when the children woke up, they could not find their sticks. But that did not stop them from playing their favorite game. They simply went out and found new sticks and sharpened them. Then they played their game all day long.

That evening, the mothers were incredibly angry. They all said, "We asked you to go down to the river to get some fish for supper. **(Draw 7, fish.)** We did not want you to play spear throwing again today. It is a waste of time. But not one of you obeyed our request. We are <u>so</u> angry about this."

The mothers were so incredibly angry, in fact, that as soon as their children were asleep, the mothers rolled the big, round rock and all the sticks that they could find into the river. **(Draw 8, more sticks and rock in river.)**

In the morning, when the children woke up, they could not find their sticks or their rock. They raced to the river. At the bottom of the river, they saw their favorite round rock and their sticks. Quickly, the children found new sticks from the woods, but they could not find another big, round rock to throw their sticks at. They decided to go back to the river to get their old rock.

They knew it was going to be hard to get their favorite rock out of the river. In frustration, they all threw their new sticks at the rock sitting on the bottom of the river.

One child misjudged the water current and did not hit the rock. Instead, his spear struck a fish that happened to be swimming by. **(Draw 9, spear through fish.)** He jumped into the river to get his spear and there was the fish, stuck fast to the end of it.

He held up the fish for everyone to see. Just then everyone got the same wonderful idea! Do you know what that idea was?

Yes, instead of throwing their spears at their big, round rock, they threw them at the fish. This was much more challenging because the fish could swim very fast.

The children made a new game to see who could spear the most fish.

That evening the children took a basket full of fish home to their mothers. What do you think the mothers said when they saw all those fish?

From then on, fishing with spears was the favorite game of the children AND their mothers.

That's my story of how spear fishing was invented.

☼ Discussion Starters

What is your favorite sport? How do you think it was invented?

(Top of page when drawing)

Sport of Spear Throwing

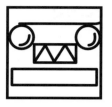

Ten Crazy Ants

Once there were ten crazy ants who lived together in a field. Lots of ants lived in this field, but these ants were known as the ten crazy ants because they were always looking for new things to do and new places to go. All the other ants liked to just stay around home, but these ants were crazy about finding new places to explore.

One bright, sunny morning, the ten crazy ants woke up and said, "Let's go exploring today." They began to get ready to go. Some of them got ready faster than others.

At eight o'clock in the morning, the first ant was ready to leave. She said, "Goodbye, fellow ants. I am going exploring in the direction of the loud noises that we heard late last night. Catch up with me when you're ready. If we don't see each other today, plan on meeting at our favorite tree at five o'clock for supper tonight."

Off went the first ant. She walked until she came to something round. She crawled all over it. She said to herself, "Wow! Look at this round, black mountain." **(Draw 1, round tire.)**

The second ant left at nine o'clock in the morning. He walked until he came to something oval. He crawled all over it. He said to himself, "Wow! Look at this long, dark cave. I better not go in it too far by myself. "It really smells!" **(Draw 2, oval exhaust pipe.)**

The third ant left at ten o'clock. She walked until she came to something square. She looked at it closely and said, "Wow! There is a picture of an ant. She looks so much like me." **(Draw 3, square rearview mirror)**

The fourth ant left at eleven o'clock. He walked until he came to something rectangular. He crawled all over it. He said to himself, "Wow! Look at this long, flat cliff overlooking the ground." **(Draw 4, rectangular bumper.)**

The fifth ant left at twelve o'clock noon. She walked until she came to something triangular. She said, "Wow! Look at these gray triangular gates." She climbed all over the gates. **(Draw 5, radiator grill with triangles.)**

The sixth ant left at one o'clock in the afternoon. He walked until he came to a tall, thin cylinder. He climbed straight up. "Wow! Look how high this tower goes. It is made out of shiny metal." **(Draw 6, cylindrical radio antenna.)**

The seventh ant left at two o'clock in the afternoon. She walked until she saw two spheres. She said, "Wow! I have found the sun and the moon! They are so bright and white!" **(Draw 7, round headlights.)**

The eighth ant left at three o'clock that afternoon. He walked until he came to a circle. He slid down it. He said, "Wow! Look at this smooth, circular slide." **(Draw 8, second tire.)**

The ninth ant left at four o'clock in the afternoon. She walked until she came to a parallelogram. She walked up on it. She said, "Wow! Look at this hard, smooth wall! I can see through it." **(Draw 9, window.)**

A little before five o'clock, the tenth ant left to meet all his friends at their favorite supper tree.

All the ants were there at the supper tree. While they were munching, they took turns telling about what they had seen that day. **(Point to all these things as you name them.)**

The first ant said, " I saw a round, black mountain." **(tire)**

The second ant said, "I saw a oval, smelly cave." **(exhaust pipe)**

The third ant said, "I saw a square picture with an ant like me in it." **(mirror)**

The fourth ant said, "I saw a long, flat cliff." **(bumper)**

The fifth ant said, "I saw a triangular gate." **(radiator grill)**

The sixth ant said, "I saw a cylindrical metal tower." **(radio antenna)**

The seventh ant said, "I saw a spherical white sun and moon." **(headlights)**

The eighth ant said, "I saw a black, circular slide." **(tire)**

The ninth ant said, "I saw a see-through wall shaped like a parallelogram." **(window)**

The tenth ant said, "You ants are all crazy! You only saw part of what you saw. I saw ALL of what you saw."

The rest of the ants said, "You're the crazy ant! You don't make any sense. Just tell us—what did YOU see?"

The tenth ant replied, "On my way to our favorite supper tree, I walked around and up and down a gently sloping hill. **(Draw 10, outline of car.)** But it wasn't really a hill. It was a...car!"

The tenth crazy ant said, "We all saw a car! Cars do have lots of interesting shapes on them, don't they?"

And that's my story of ten crazy ants!

☼ Discussion Starters

Think up your own object that the ants or another group of insects or animals can discover. What is the object? How do they describe it?

(Top of page when drawing)

Ten Crazy Ants

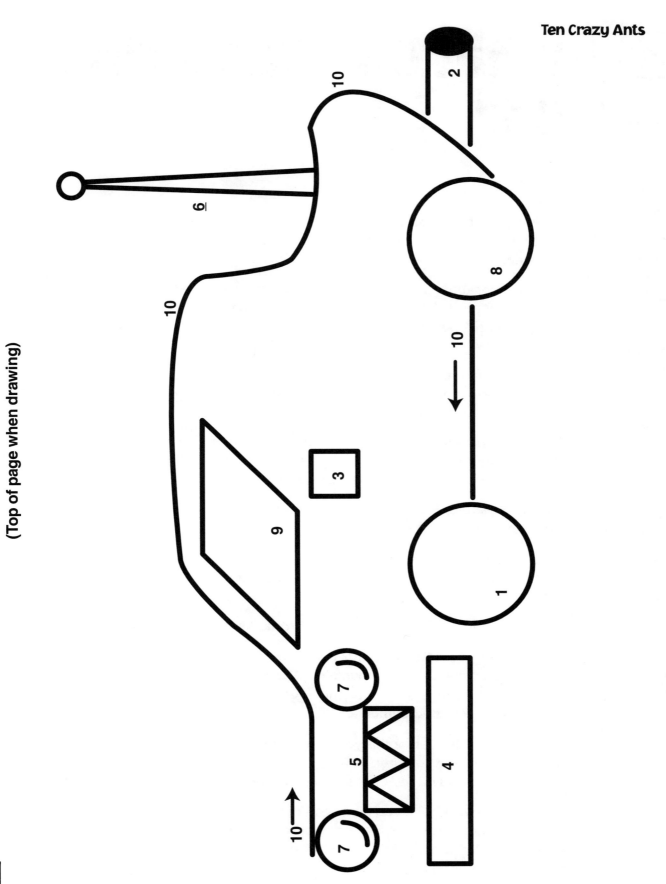

What Can Catherine Do?

Have you ever been bored on a Saturday morning? You don't know quite what to do, and none of your toys or games interest you. That has happened to all of us at one time or another, hasn't it?

This is a story about a girl named Catherine who was bored one Saturday morning. She said to her dad, "Can I go with you to the zoo this morning? I want to help you take care of the snakes, and I'd love to see your new boa constrictor." **(Draw 1, curly slide.)**

Catherine's dad replied, "I'm not going in to work today, honey. It's Saturday and I thought we could do something special together. What else would you like to do today?"

"I really do want to go with you to your office at the zoo. Being in charge of the snakes must be a really neat job. Tell me again, what is your title as snake expert?" asked Catherine.

"I am a herpetologist, that's a person who studies snakes and other reptiles," answered her dad.

"That's right, a herpetologist," said Catherine. "I am going to be a herpetologist too, when I grow up. May we go see the lizards at the zoo today?"

Her dad answered, "Not today. Think of something else to do."

"Well, would you take me skiing? I've always wanted to glide down those long ski slopes in the mountains. **(Draw 2, slide.)** You said you would take me someday when I got bigger and stronger. Now I'm bigger and stronger," said Catherine.

"The ski season is over for this year, but I know that by next year you will be even bigger and stronger. I'll take you then. Besides, the ski lodge is already closed and locked up." said Dad. **(Draw 3, first tower.)**

"Okay, I'll snow ski with you next year! But could you take me to the mountains today anyway? That's one of your favorite hobbies isn't it? I'd be really, really careful climbing up the rocky mountainside with you," Catherine said hopefully. **(Draw 4, steps.)**

"I know you would, honey, but in order to do the type of mountain climbing that I do, a person must take special classes and learn how to use ropes and special equipment," said her dad. "It also takes hours of practice to climb those steep mountain peaks." **(Draw 5, second tower.)** "Let's think of something easy that we can do together right now that would be fun."

"How about if you take me up in your airplane? It is so exciting when we take off and land on the long airport runway!" suggested Catherine. **(Draw 6, swing.)**

"Great idea, Catherine, but let's do that next weekend. My partner has the airplane today. Remember, we take turns using the airplane," said Dad. "Let's think of something else we can do."

"I know, let's go fishing! I love scooping the fish out of the water with our big fishing net," yelled Catherine. **(Draw 7, net.)**

"Do you know where our fishing poles are?" asked Dad.

"Oh, no!" answered Catherine. "We left them in the shed at Grandma's lake cottage. I guess we can't go fishing. Now what do we do?"

Catherine's dad again named all the things that they could not do. **(Point to each thing as you name it.)** "Let's see here. We cannot go to see the snakes **(1)**. We cannot go skiing **(2 and 3)**. We cannot go mountain climbing **(4 and 5)**. We cannot use the airport runways **(6)**. We cannot use our big fishing net **(7)**. What can we do?"

As Dad pointed to all the things they could not do, Catherine got an idea. **(Draw 8, rectangle.)** She took a marker and connected all the things that they couldn't do together and saw that it was really a. . .

Yes, that's right, a playground!

Catherine said, "Let's go to the playground. It's fun and easy for us both to do."

So the next Saturday that you are bored, do what Catherine and her dad did—go to the playground.

☼ Discussion Starters

What do you like to do on Saturdays and Sundays? Have you ever done some of the things that Catherine has? What else can you do?

What Can Catherine Do?

(Top of page when drawing)

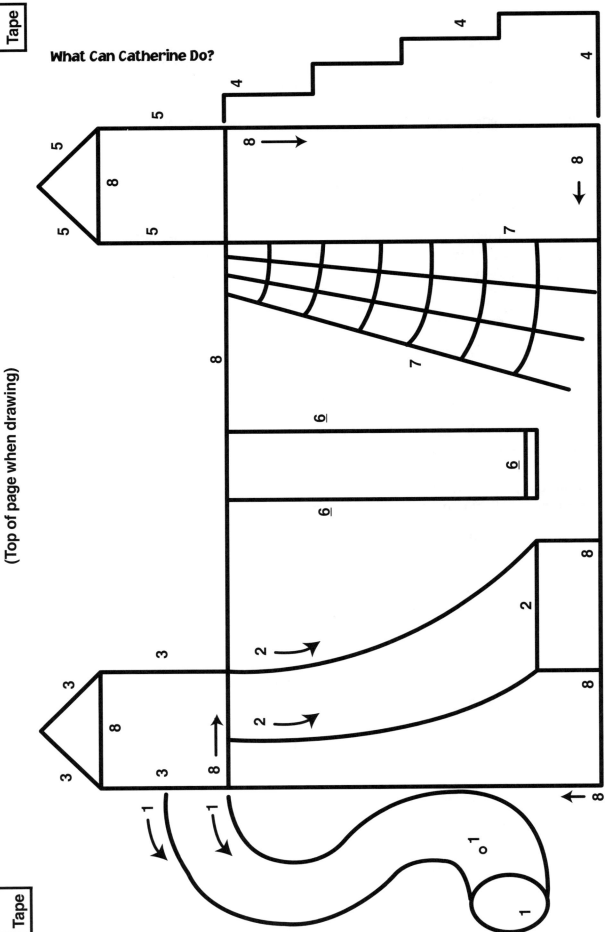

(Note: Lightly draw rectangle 8 to help in placement of playground components.)

Which Flower?

A King Solomon Tale

Far ago, there lived a king who was famous for his goodness and his wisdom. His subjects often asked his advice when they had a particularly difficult problem. It seemed King Solomon had an answer for even the most difficult of questions.

In a land not far from King Solomon's kingdom ruled the Queen of Sheba. The queen desperately wanted to ask the king a question that he could not answer. Then she could show everyone that she was as wise as King Solomon.

She searched for the hardest riddle that she could find. Finally, the queen decided on one question that she was sure no one, not even King Solomon himself, could answer.

The queen told her royal craftsmen and magicians to create beautiful flowers of brightly colored silk. She ordered her royal perfume makers to give each flower its own true scent. The silk daisies smelled like real daisies, and the silk roses smelled like real roses. **(Draw 1, flower petals only. Use bright color such as orange or pink.)**

The craftsmen worked for many, many days and finally created the most beautiful silk flowers. They had delicate colors and scents so real that no one could tell they were artificial. There were so many flowers that they completely filled the royal palace hall. People came from miles around to see such beautiful works of art. Even King Solomon came.

On the day of his arrival, the queen herself went out into the royal garden and picked a single lovely daisy. She carefully carried it in to the palace hall and placed it in with the fabulous fakes. **(Draw 2, flower stem and leaves. Use green marker.)**

Then she invited the king into the palace hall and said to him, "Most honored and wise king, in this room I have placed many beautiful flowers, each as lovely as the next. Although it is hard to believe, these flowers are not real. They were made of silk by my finest craftsmen."

The king agreed, "Your flowers are indeed lovely and very real-looking."

The queen replied, "Thank you. But I must tell you that this morning I went out to the royal garden and picked one flower, one <u>real</u> flower. I put the real flower in with these fabulous fakes. Now I know that you, King Solomon, in all your wisdom will be able to quickly find the real flower."

The king realized that this was indeed what he must do and do quickly. He walked up and down each row of flowers, carefully examining each flower.

Then he returned to the queen's side, and she looked at him expectantly, "Well? Well?" she asked.

King Solomon replied, "Well, your royal craftsmen and magicians have done a superb job of making all these flowers look so real. My deepest compliments to them. I hope you don't mind me asking, but I was wondering if…"

The queen interrupted him. "Oh, no! You cannot ask me anything! You must tell me which is the real flower. Surely, you in all your wisdom do not need any hints from me."

The king quietly replied, "I was only going to ask you if I might sit down for a bit. I am suddenly not feeling well."

Realizing her lack of hospitality, the queen was quite embarrassed. She hadn't even noticed that the king was looking rather warm. She clapped her hands loudly and, immediately, two servants appeared. She ordered, "Bring a chair for the king." The servants came running with a chair.

The king sat down. He put his head in his hands. He really looked quite ill. The queen said, "Please forgive my lack of hospitality. Are you feeling better now?"

"Yes, somewhat, but I am still so hot. If I could trouble you for a glass of water…" the king whispered.

Again, the queen realized that she had failed in her duties as a hostess. She clapped her hands loudly and two more servants appeared. She ordered, "Bring some water for the king." The servants came running with a pitcher of cold water. The king drank a glass of water but still looked overheated.

The queen asked again, "Are you feeling better now?"

The king said," Yes, somewhat."

Determined not to be embarrassed a third time, she clapped her hands loudly again. Immediately, two more servants appeared. She yelled, "Can't you servants see that the king needs some fresh air?" The servants ran to open all the windows. **(Draw window frame around flower. Use black marker.)**

The queen asked again, "Are you feeling better now? Now can you answer my riddle?"

Slowly, the king stood up. He looked around carefully. Then, *slowly*, he walked over to a table of flowers. Carefully, he bent over and picked out the daisy, the only <u>real</u> flower in the hall. He carried it over to the queen and presented it to her with a gracious bow.

The queen was so astonished that the king had discovered the real flower that she was unable to speak.

Question: How do you think the king was able to identify the real flower?

Allow time for listeners to make answers. Give hints if necessary, such as "Yes, it has to do with the open windows. Yes, the king had some help. His help came from something that flew in the windows. **(Finish window frame.)**

Answer: When the windows were opened, a honeybee flew in and landed on the real flower. The king knew that the honeybee would land only on the real flower. **(Fold paper up and draw the bee's body. Add eyes, mouth and antennae to top flower petal.)**

Do you think the king really was hot? Why did he pretend to be hot?

The moral of this story? Even the smallest among us has wisdom to offer.

$\heartsuit\heartsuit\heartsuit\heartsuit\heartsuit\heartsuit$

☼ Discussion Starters

What other animals or insects know things that people don't know? How do they know this? Have you heard the term "instinct"? Let's discuss its meaning.

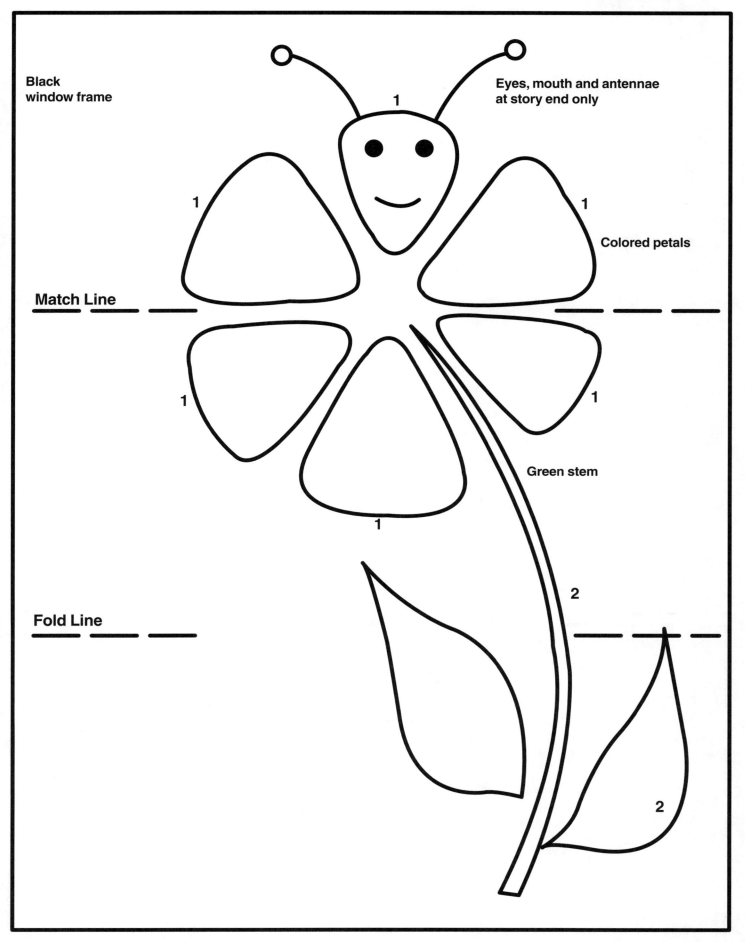

Black
window frame

Eyes, mouth and antennae
at story end only

Colored petals

Match Line

Green stem

Fold Line

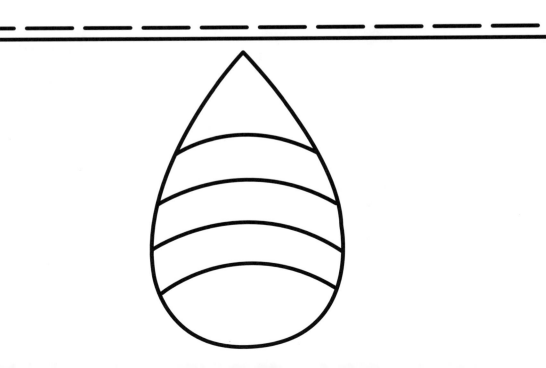

Why Giraffes Have Long necks

Did you know that, far ago, giraffes looked like this? **(Draw 1, round giraffe.)** They were beautiful, roly-poly, cream-colored, gentle animals who liked to eat sweet things and organize everything. Here's the story of how giraffes changed from this roly-poly creature into the majestic, long-necked creatures that we know today.

One day, two giraffes, Chris and her friend Dave, went out walking. They came upon the molasses tree. It looked like this. **(Draw 2, tree trunk under giraffe. Color brown spots on tree and giraffe.)**

"Dave," said Chris, "I think that this tree is in the wrong place. I think I should move it."

"Chris," said Dave, "you can't move the molasses tree. This is where it wants to grow."

"Yes, Dave, but all the rest of the molasses trees are growing over there, and this one belongs with them," replied Chris. "I think I'll just move it so it can be with the rest of the molasses trees."

"Chris, you are crazy. You cannot reorganize trees. Besides, this one looks really sticky. See all that molasses dripping from the leaves and trunk? Don't even touch it. You will get stuck," Dave said.

But before Dave had even finished speaking, Chris had wrapped all four of her feet around the tree and was pulling with all her might. She began yelling, "Come and help me, Dave!"

Dave said, "Help you move the tree or help you get unstuck?"

"What a joker you are!" laughed Chris, and she stuck her tongue out at him. **(Draw 3, tongue and head of giraffe touching tree.)** Then she said, "Actually, I think I am stuck in this sticky, gooey molasses. I do need you to pull me off. This sweet stuff really tastes good, though." She began swallowing molasses. **(Draw 4, neck with brown spots.)**

Dave started pulling on Chris. **(Begin drawing 5, giraffe body and legs.)**

"Pull harder, Dave! I'm really stuck!" she yelled.

He pulled and he pulled and he pulled. He pulled on her legs, he pulled on her neck and he even pulled on her tail!

"Oh no, I'm stretching, all of me is stretching!" Chris said.

By the time Dave had finally gotten Chris unstuck from the molasses tree, her legs, her tail, and her neck looked like this. **(Point to your new drawing of giraffe.)**

"Look at me now! I'm all stretched out. I don't look at all like I did before. I have such a long neck and such long legs and such a long tail. Look at all of these brown spots on me from the molasses. **(Draw 6, brown spots.)** You know, I always wanted to be tall and slender with a beautiful fur coat. I like the new me!" exclaimed Chris.

"I think you look great. But what about the sticky molasses tree? You did not get it moved yet. Are you going to try again to move it?" asked Dave.

"Chris answered, "Well, I guess not ALL the trees have to be in the same place. This tree can be different. We really don't have to organize all of the trees. I'm glad the tree is where it is, and I'm glad I am who I am. Now I can reach up with my long neck to eat all of the tastiest, juiciest leaves on the tops of the trees. I think I'll stay away from the sticky molasses trees, though. My neck is long enough."

All of the other giraffes liked Chris's new look so much that they decided to change their looks also. They stretched their necks, legs and tails and ate brown molasses, creating spots on themselves to look like the giraffes that we know today.

$$O_o O_o O O_o O O_o$$

☼ Discussion Starters

There are many stories of why animals look like they do today. Find one in the library and create a picture to draw while you are telling the story.

Why Giraffes Have Long Necks

Why Rabbits Have Long Ears

An Russian Folktale

Far ago, Rabbit and Goat were arguing about who could do the best tricks.

Rabbit said, "I can jump much higher than you, Goat. Watch this." Rabbit jumped right over a bush with one leap, and then he leaped again and cleared a fence!

Goat was impressed. He said, "That's really great, Rabbit."

"Oh, yeah! And I could even jump over that tree if I wanted to, but I'm a little tired just now," Rabbit boasted.

Goat leaned against the tree and tried to think of something that he could do that Rabbit could not do. Finally, Goat said, " I can put my front feet here. **(Draw 1, eyes.)** I can put my back feet here. **(Draw 2, inside of ears.)** Then I can bend my head down and knock off that large tree branch. See that one sticking out on the side?" **(Draw 3, right back foot.)**

"Cool," said Rabbit. "But how are you going to do that?"

Goat said, "I'm going to use my wonderful horns. Watch this." **(Draw 4, rabbit's front feet.)**

Goat lowered his head, got a running start and ran smack into the tree branch. **(Draw 5, right side of body.)** He didn't knock the branch off, but he splintered it in two places. **(Draw 6, toe lines.)**

Rabbit was impressed, but he didn't show it. Instead, he said, "Oh, I can do that too. Not only that, I can jump over the pond first and then knock off that other tree branch."

Goat said, "I really don't think you should do that, Rabbit. I couldn't even do it. You might hurt yourself. You don't have strong horns like I do. You just have those tender little ears."

But Rabbit didn't listen. He said, "If you can do it, I can do it. You just watch this."

Rabbit lowered his head and started to run. He jumped over the pond. **(Draw 7, circle for head.)** He ran straight toward the tree branch as fast as he could. **(Draw 8, left side of body.)** He rammed his head into the branch as hard as he could. **(Draw 9, left back foot.)**

Rabbit did not knock the tree branch off or even split it. **(Draw 10, toe lines.)** Instead, he had rammed his head into the tree so hard that he bounced off it. Now his head was stuck down in between his shoulders.

Rabbit began to yell, "Help! Help! Someone get my head out. Goat, come here and get me out." Rabbit yelled and yelled.

Goat came running as fast as he could. "Just hang on, Rabbit. I'll get your head free." Goat began pulling on Rabbit's ears. He was hoping that Rabbit's head would pop out that way.

But Rabbit yelled, "Stop, stop! You are hurting my ears!"

Just then, Rabbit's head popped back out from his shoulders. **(Turn drawing upside down to reveal picture of Rabbit. Quickly add 11, whiskers, and 12, mouth, to face.)** Here is Rabbit's head.

But you know, Goat had pulled so hard on Rabbit's ears that he stretched them. Instead of cute, short little ears, his ears now looked like this. **(Draw 13, long ears.)** From that day forward, rabbits always grew their ears long. And today, rabbits still have long ears.

☼ Discussion Starters

Can you think of another explanation to the question, "Why do rabbits have long ears?"

Why Rabbits Have Long Ears

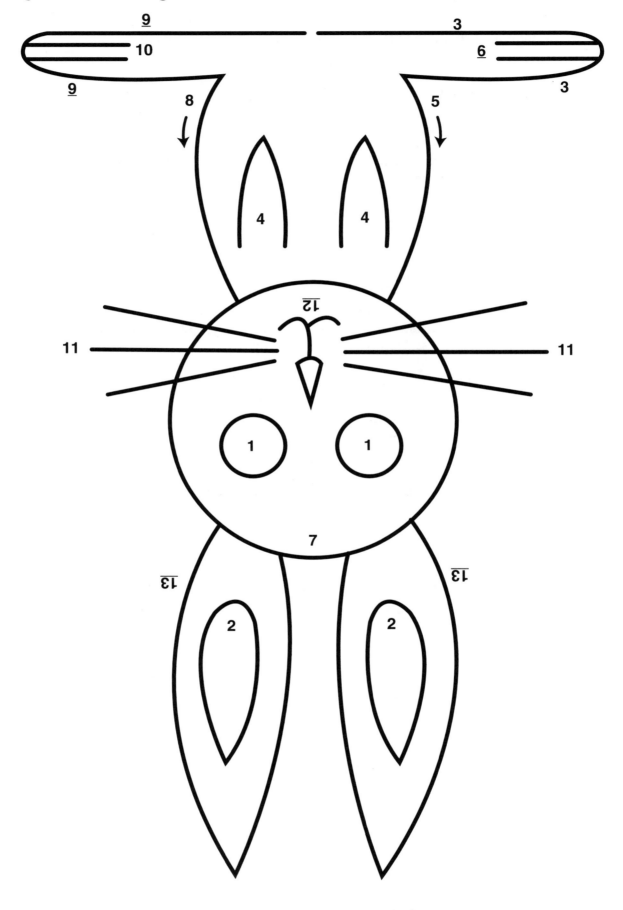